Theaetetus

PLATO

Theaetetus

Edited, with Introduction, by
Bernard Williams

Translated by
M. J. Levett

Revised by
Myles Burnyeat

HACKETT PUBLISHING COMPANY

Indianapolis/Cambridge

Plato: ca. 428–347 B.C.

Cover design by Listenberger Design & Associates
Interior design by Dan Kirklin

For further information, please address
Hackett Publishing Company, Inc.
P.O. Box 44937
Indianapolis, Indiana 46244-0937

Library of Congress Cataloging-in-Publication Data

Plato.
　　[Theaetetus. English]
　　Theaetetus/Plato; edited, with introduction by Bernard Williams;
　　translated by M.J. Levett; revised by Myles Burnyeat.
　　　　p.　　cm.
　　Includes bibliographical references.
　　ISBN 0-87220-159-7　ISBN 0-87220-158-9 (pbk).
　　1. Knowledge, Theory of.　I. Williams, Bernard Arthur Owen.
　　II. Levett, M.J.　III.　Burnyeat, Myles　IV. Title.
　　B386.A5L48　1992
　　121—dc20　　　　　　　　　　　　　　　　　　　92-28261
　　　　　　　　　　　　　　　　　　　　　　　　　　　CIP

CONTENTS

INTRODUCTION

Like all of Plato's dialogues, the *Theaetetus* presents a conversation that did not actually take place. The dialogue form is not meant to give an historical record; it is a style of writing that enables Plato to explore philosophical questions in ways more vivid and more intellectually flexible than are available to a treatise. Above all, the dialogue form enables Plato not to speak in his own person. The leading figure in the dialogues, except for some of the last that he wrote, is Plato's teacher Socrates. The ideas which Socrates expresses in the dialogues, or helps to construct in conversation with the other characters, are not necessarily ideas that were known to the historical Socrates, and in many of the dialogues, including the *Theaetetus*, the materials of the discussion are quite certainly Plato's.

Questions are raised not only by Socrates' presence, but also by Plato's absence. We should not assume that there is a straight-forward route from any given dialogue to Plato's beliefs. We are used to the idea that philosophers have theories or even systems, which they lay before us in articles or monographs. Reading Plato's dialogues, we may easily think that they are just a literary device for putting across opinions which he might, if he wished, have expressed more directly. There are a few dialogues of which that is a fair description; in some the form of dialogue is almost abandoned. But the very fact that in some cases Plato is clearly talking to us through the dialogue should make us question the assumption that he is always doing so.

Hardly anyone now thinks that all Plato's dialogues, or all except the earliest, express the *same* theory, roughly that of the *Republic*. Most people accept that Plato developed, questioned, and even perhaps changed his theories. But we still need to guard against the idea that every time Plato wrote a dialogue he was act-ing as curator of his own system, keeping it in place or monitoring its developments. Plato certainly had some systematic beliefs, and still more some guiding metaphysical and ethical concerns, which are variously and powerfully expressed in his work. He has always been regarded as one of the greatest Western philoso-phers, by some people as the greatest of them all. Notwithstanding the achievements of his remarkable predecessors whose writings are lost to us (several are mentioned in this dialogue), he virtually invented the subject, philosophy. He was the first to express many distinctively philosophical questions and concerns; in the *Theaetetus*, he explores in an intense and closely argued way ideas which have shaped the ways in which people have subsequently discussed what knowledge might be, and whether we can have any. But as well as explicit philosophical content, Plato lays before us in his dialogues various attitudes which also belong to philosophy, such as curiosity, puzzlement, and intellectual surprise. His characters may be excited, bored, confused, or impressed; they take up, in such moods, all sorts of analogies, metaphors, stories, and models (for instance, of the human mind); they learn something from them, and often then throw them away. The dialogues, very often, embody these processes of inquiry—they do not merely present, in coded form, its results. If we are going to get the most from reading one of Plato's dialogues, we have to keep in close touch with its tone, sustaining a sense of what is a joke, what is merely provisional, what is being tried out or tried on.

The *Theaetetus* is a dialogue to which this advice particularly applies. Socrates reiterates a theme familiar from Plato's earliest dialogues, that he himself knows nothing, and that he is merely there to discuss and criticize other people's ideas, and to help them formulate them; it is here that, in a famous image, he compares his role to that of a midwife (150). On its central question, 'what is knowledge?', the dialogue's results are negative, but it is not supposed that we have learned nothing in disposing of the various answers which are proposed in the course of the argument. Moreover, the various answers themselves, as we shall see, are not merely suggestions randomly elicited by the question. They speak to various important preconceptions, and they help to identify theoretical problems which will have to be faced in any later discussion of knowledge.

Many scholars have assumed that there is definite doctrine to be gathered from between the lines of the dialogue. Partly, this is because it is agreed that the dialogue was written after the *Phaedo*, the *Symposium*, and the *Republic*, with their ambitious metaphysical speculations about a changeless order of 'Forms' separate from the world of ordinary material happening, and it is felt that the *Theaetetus* must have something to say about those matters since it concerns knowledge (which in the *Republic* is confined to the Forms), and indeed seems to express in the Digression (172–177) some of the same attitudes to philosophy, contrasted with the world of practical affairs, as are to be found in these dialogues. Indeed, there is a reading of the first and longest Part of the dialogue, discussing the idea that knowledge is perception, which represents the argument of that Part as relying on the kind of view of the material world that is to be found in the *Republic*.[1]

Whether we accept that reading or not, we should not assume that because there are theoretical commitments in the offing and Plato here refers to various philosophical theories, the dialogue is all the time trying to get some doctrine across to us, as opposed to making us think about the issues. Moreover, as Myles Burnyeat has said:

> . . . readers of the *Theaetetus* are required to contribute more and more as the dialogue proceeds. As I see it, your task in Part I is to *find* the meaning in the text and follow the argument to a satisfactory conclusion. In Part II you are challenged to *respond* to the meaning in the text by overcoming the problems and paradoxes that it leaves unresolved. In Part III the task is nothing less than to *create* from the text a meaning which will solve the problem of knowledge.

The three Parts of the dialogue discuss, at very different lengths, three different suggestions for what knowledge is: that it is perception, that it is true judgement, and that it is true judgement together with 'an account'. Before the first of these ideas is taken up and submitted to a long examination, Socrates helps to set up the inquiry with a demand for a general account of the notion in question: It is no good giving, as Theaetetus first does, a list of kinds of knowledge, because that will not tell us what *makes* those things kinds of knowledge. When Socrates makes this

1. In his introduction to Miss Levett's translation, Burnyeat calls this Reading A, as opposed to another, Reading B, which understands the use of the "flux" material in this section as part of a long *reductio ad absurdum*, not something that Plato himself believes about the material world. Burnyeat, very carefully laying out the alternatives, leaves the decision between them (or yet another) to the reader. Anyone who wants to arrive at a serious conclusion about the meaning of the dialogue should work his or her way through Burnyeat's invaluable discussion of the arguments, both here and throughout the dialogue. The present, very much shorter, Introduction is indebted at several points to his, while both have their origins in past discussions which he and I have had about the dialogue.

The quotation in the following paragraph is from the Preface to his Introduction, pp. xii–xiii. See Myles Burnyeat, *The Theaetetus of Plato*, with text translated by M. J. Levett, revised by Myles Burnyeat (Hackett: Indianapolis & Cambridge, 1990).

demand, as he does in several other Platonic dialogues, it is often objected by modern critics that, for many of our notions, there is no reason to suppose that we can give a definition which captures their various applications. In trying to understand the ways in which many different things can be called a 'game', for instance, or a 'machine', or 'honest', or 'natural', it is unlikely that we shall get far by looking for the kind of neat formula that pairs 'vixen' with 'female fox'. Why should we expect there to be one for knowledge? The general point is well taken. But, equally, there is good reason to wonder whether Socrates, at least in this dialogue, is really looking for such a formula. The first suggestion offered by Theaetetus and taken up for discussion is that knowledge is perception, and this is certainly not a definitional formula. For one thing, Socrates makes it quite clear later on (165d) that it is not to be tested by merely considering whether 'perceive' and related terms can be substituted for 'know': It will not count against the proposal, for instance, that one can be said to see or hear dimly or faintly, but not to know something dimly or faintly. Moreover, it is immediately obvious that an identification of knowledge with perception will not fit the examples of knowledge that came up when Theaetetus was assembling a list. Those were all cases of a skill or a kind of expertise, and they are not kinds of perception. Indeed, the relations of expertise to knowledge as perception will turn out, rather later in Part I, to be altogether problematic.

The list is rejected for a more general reason, that it will not give any insight into the nature of knowledge. The idea that knowledge is perception is worth considering as possibly giving insight (though not if it is treated simply as a definition). Socrates examines the idea by working it up into a theory. First he says (151e) that Theaetetus' suggestion is what used to be maintained by Protagoras, a famous teacher who was a contemporary of Socrates and who appears in one of Plato's most brilliant dialogues, which bears his name. Protagoras claimed that 'man is the measure of all things', a saying which is here taken to mean that each man is the measure of the things that are *for him:* in the sense that if, for instance, one person finds the wind cold and another finds it warm, the right thing to say is that the wind is cold for the one and is warm for the other. If we say this, relativizing the statement made by each person to his or her own perception, neither person can be wrong. There is no room for error, since no claim is being made beyond what later philosophy was to call the 'immediate experience' of each person. Indeed, it is wrong to imply that there is any such thing as the state of the wind *in itself*. Protagoras' thought is that the wind is cold for one person and warm for another, and that is all there is to it. We may say in ordinary speech that the wind is 'really' warm, but that is at best a statistical judgement, to the effect that it is warm for more people than not. (There is an important question, to which we shall come back, whether Protagoras, sticking to his preferred forms of speech, can in fact make those statistical claims.)

From this, it is an easy step—one needs to ask, when reading the dialogue, how easy a step it is—to saying that everything which really happens can be reported simply by statements of immediate experience: Everything that is, in any sense, is for some individual. Individuals themselves, moreover, exist only as participants in these perceptual encounters. Understood in this way, Protagoras' doctrine turns out to be a version of the theory associated with Heracleitus (a philosopher who flourished around 500 B.C., whose work survives only in obscure but often deeply impressive fragments), that 'everything is in flux': nothing *is* anything without qualification. So Socrates is able to say (160d) that three theories come to the same thing: the view of Heracleitus and others, 'that all things flow like streams; of Protagoras, wisest of men, that man is the measure of all things; and of Theaetetus that, things being so, knowledge proves to be perception.' The central problem about the meaning of Part I of the *Theaetetus* is to decide the sense in which these three things do 'come to the same thing'.

In the course of reaching this conclusion, Socrates questions the basis on which people conventionally suppose that some of their experiences better tell them how things 'really' are than others do: the experiences they have when they are well, for instance, as opposed to those they have when they are sick, or waking experiences rather than those had in dreams. Indeed, most radically, he asks how one can tell whether one is awake or dreaming, and with this question he helped to start a skeptical tradition of questioning which, above all through the influence of Descartes, has continued into modern philosophy.

Developing the Heracleitean aspect of the view, Socrates brings in a theory about 'slow' and 'quick' motions. A modern critic will want to know whether this is a physical theory—a sort of scientific hypothesis—or, alternatively, a metaphysical model, a vivid way of representing the implications of sticking to Protagorean certainties. This question did not present itself to Plato in quite that form, and it is probably better to leave it to be settled in the light of other interpretative answers one needs to give. Above all, one needs to decide whether Plato brings in the Heracleitean material as something that he himself believes about the material world, or whether it is elicited simply as a consequence of the Protagorean view, itself constructed as offering the only sense in which perception could be knowledge—because immediate perception is the only kind of perception that, like knowledge, has a content which, necessarily, is true. (Plato gives several opportunities to ask whether knowledge and immediate perception do have some such feature in common.) If one takes the second line, the argument that leads to the rejection of the Heracleitean view constitutes a long *reductio ad absurdum* of Theaetetus' suggestion. It is not even plausible (this argument will go) that knowledge is perception, unless immediate perception is meant, to which Protagoras' maxim applies, but if one sticks to what is determined by that maxim, one has a Heracleitean world, and if the world is Heracleitean, no language or thought is possible (181–83).

It may be asked why, on this line, Protagoras has to lead to Heracleitus. Even if the only *knowledge* lies in the indubitable data of immediate perception—'hot for me now'—might we not be able to think of enduring things, such as material objects and people, as the objects merely of belief? There is more than one way of approaching that question, but Plato's outlook on it is probably shaped by an important assumption, one that has been shared in one form or another by many subsequent philosophers: that knowledge must be self-sufficient, and cannot need anything weaker than itself. If Protagoras' statements offer all the knowledge there is, they cannot presuppose an understanding of the world which rests in mere belief. If Protagorean statements constitute all the knowledge there is, then we must be able to understand the idea that what those statements present as a world is all the world there is.

Before he reaches his eventual refutation of the Heracleitean element, Socrates engages in some complicated maneuvres against the Protagorean element by itself. After rejecting some charges against Protagoras as purely *ad hominem*, he isolates the powerful objection that Protagoras' theory cannot account for its own claim to be true; indeed, if others think the theory false, they cannot be wrong in thinking this. (This is one of the first uses of a pattern of argument that has often been used since, by which a philosopher's theory is applied to itself.) It has been objected that in this argument Socrates falls back on an unrelativized sense of 'true' which Protagoras' theory has eliminated, but that objection raises some deeper questions. Protagoras' formulae did not rely on deploying a relativized sense of *true*. What were relativized were the perceptual terms, such as 'hot' '*It is hot* is true for me' got its content by meaning 'It is hot for me'. In the light of this, Socrates' objection has force, because it is quite unclear what Protagoras might be doing in asserting things such as a philosophical theory, which cannot be expressed in such terms. He has, for instance, no way of claiming that someone who comes to accept his theory will be replacing false views with true ones.

At this point in the dialogue, it is indeed suggested that Protagoras might dispense with this claim altogether, and say instead that he can help people to replace states of mind that are less nice (for them) with states of mind that will be nicer (for them). But in reply to this, in one of Plato's most brilliant insights, Socrates points out that any claim to be able to do such a thing involves predictions, and a prediction about future Protagorean certainties cannot itself be a Protagorean certainty: no-one possesses a 'a criterion within himself' (178c) of what *will* be, even of what will be for himself. (There has been earlier, at 166b, a suggestion that Protagoras might have more success with statements about the past, reducing memories to present impressions.) In the case of the future (and the same applies, we may add, to those 'statistical' questions of *how many* people are having certain kinds of experience) nothing can eliminate the fact that two people can have conflicting beliefs, and there is nothing such as immediate experience to guarantee that one rather than the other is right. In these cases, unlike that of immediate experience, the parties are symmetrically related to the subject matter of the judgement—for neither of them is it peculiarly 'his'. It is precisely in such cases that there is room for expertise, and because of this, as Socrates makes clear, the objection against Protagoras, that he destroys his own claims to be wiser than others, is not merely personal rhetoric. Rather, by removing any realm for expertise, he removes one of the most important applications of the notion of knowledge. It begins to look as though, when at the beginning we turned away from kinds of expertise to immediate perceptual experience and its subjective certainties, we may have turned in the wrong direction.

Before we leave the first Part of the dialogue, another argument is offered against the claim that knowledge is perception, independently of the long discussion that ran through Protagoras and Heracleitus. This argument, which again has had an immensely important influence on later philosophy, rests on the idea that each sense can grasp items only of a certain kind, as sight relates to colors, hearing to sounds, and so forth. But knowledge requires concepts that are not tied in this way to any of the senses, concepts such as sameness, difference, and being. By which of the senses could we gather that a sound is something different from a color? Yet this is certainly something we know, and indeed everything we know involves concepts of this nonsensory kind. So knowledge is not perception, and this, at any rate, is something we have come to understand, as Socrates says. There are other things, as well, that we can come to understand in thinking through the long and wonderfully subtle route that has led to this conclusion.

The dialogue now takes a new turn, and Theaetetus offers a different suggestion: that knowledge is true judgement. This suggestion is also refuted, at the end of Part II (200–201), with a very swift argument which is a paradigm of the arguments still used to make this point. Someone may have a true belief about a certain matter, but it may be sheer luck that his belief is true—acquiring it as he did, he might just as well have acquired a false one. If this is so, his true belief does not count as knowledge. This is Plato's argument, and it is conclusive, even though it is not entirely clear from the example what contrast Plato has in mind between sound and unsound sources of belief. His scene is a law court, in which a lawyer or orator persuades the jury of something which may indeed be true, but where the conditions prevent their coming to a sound judgement on the matter. Does Plato want to emphasize the distinction between firsthand experience, such as an eye-witness might have, and mere secondhand testimony? Or rather the distinction between a thorough argument and a hasty, superficial one? The distinction does not make much difference to the use of the example for this particular purpose. It would make a difference if Plato were to try to develop an account of knowledge by building directly on such examples, as many modern theorists do, but as we shall see, he does not try to do so.

The jury example, which refutes the suggestion that knowledge is true belief, takes only a page at the very end of Part II. Almost all of the Part is devoted to a preliminary question, whether there can be such a thing as false judgement. Two lines of argument are introduced to suggest that false judgement may be impossible. One of them (188–89) is to the effect that false judgement must involve 'thinking what is not', which is hard to distinguish from thinking nothing, which, in turn, must be equivalent to not thinking at all. This kind of argument is not pursued in the *Theaetetus*, but is discussed at length in its successor dialogue, the *Sophist*; so, too, are the views of Parmenides and others already mentioned (180–81, 183–84), who held that everything is, in some sense, one, and that there can be no change or difference in the world. The *Sophist* displays, among other things, Plato's insight that these two issues, of falsehood and of change, are closely related to one another, and that both demand a close examination of ideas of 'being'.

The *Theaetetus* itself pursues only the other of the two problems about false judgement which it mentions, one that centers on the idea of taking, or mistaking, one thing for another. The argument is that this must be impossible. One cannot make a mistake about something one does not know (how could one even think of it?), and from this it follows that one cannot mistake two things one does not know for each other, nor something one does not know for something one knows. But, further, one cannot mistake for each other two things one knows, since this would be enough to show that one did not know them: If someone could say to himself, and believe it, 'Theaetetus is Theodorus', then he would literally not know what he was talking about. But of everything it is true that either one knows it or one does not know it, so these are all the conceivable combinations; so nothing can be mistaken for anything else. The upshot of the argument, in effect, is that it is a necessary condition of mistaking two items for one another that one should know them both, but this is also a sufficient condition of knowing them apart—that is to say, of not mistaking them.

Faced with this puzzle, Socrates introduces a possibility which helps the discussion to make a little progress. The assumptions of the argument are not quite true, because one may mistake something one perceives for something one knows, and the thing or person one perceives may be either known or unknown to one. Thus I may take someone I see in the distance for Theaetetus, who is known to me, and the person I see may in fact be someone else I know, such as Theodorus, or it may be a stranger. In such a case, I can make a mistake. Socrates works out all (or almost all) the possibilities that this new idea permits, illustrating it with a model of the mind as a wax block which takes and preserves images of items one has previously perceived. (The wax block is here a model just of memory, and not, as it became in later philosophy, of perception.) When I later perceive something, I may fit that perception to an image on my Block, and in this process there lies the possibility of mistake.

However, this model cannot be enough. We can make mistakes about things that are not perceived at all. Thus someone who asks what seven and five add up to may, if he is bad at arithmetic, think that the answer is eleven rather than twelve, and this mistake cannot be explained in terms of the Block. So a second model is introduced, of an aviary or birdcage. As one acquires knowledge of the numbers, one comes to possess, as it were, birds of knowledge which enter the cage of the mind. Seeking the answer to a given question, one tries to grasp the right bird, and one may grasp the wrong one, as the person does who thinks that eleven, rather than twelve, is what seven and five add up to.

With the Aviary, Plato introduces a distinction which is very important to the theory of knowledge, between dispositional knowledge and knowledge in action, represented by the model in terms of merely possessing a bird in the cage as opposed to holding it in one's hand. This distinction (which was later expressed by Aristotle in terms of having knowledge and using it) is useful, but it does not solve the present problem. If there is a puzzle of how one can take one thing one knows for another thing one knows, it arises just as much with the birds in the model—the Aviary has simply replaced one mistake with another. It is no help, either, to add to the Aviary, as Theaetetus rather desperately suggests, 'pieces of ignorance': That raises the same problem again, and some others as well.

Scholars have wondered how the Block and the Aviary are to be reconciled with things that Plato says elsewhere about knowledge, perception, and our grasp of arithmetic. These worries are pointless. The models are designed to deal with a specific question, and we should concentrate on the aspects of them that are relevant to that question. Thus 'having in one's aviary the bird that is the knowledge of eleven' merely represents the capacity to think of the number eleven, and we need not bother here with such matters as the metaphysical status of numbers. We are left with enough questions, even when we leave aside the irrelevant ones, and each of the models has given rise to much discussion. With the Aviary, for instance, are birds corresponding to seven and to five involved in the mistake that Socrates describes? Is there a separate bird labelled 'the sum of seven and five'? The best answer to these questions seems to be that only birds corresponding to eleven and to twelve are mentioned, and Plato leaves us with the unsolved problem of how one of them can be mistaken for the other, as it seems it must be if 'eleven' is thought to answer the question 'What are seven and five?'.

A question that needs to be considered is whether Plato intends to leave us with any positive result from the Wax Block. Does it make a contribution to understanding mistakes that involve perception, and fail only to the extent that it cannot explain others?

Or does its failure to explain others mean that it gives too shallow a view even of the mistakes involving perception? Here we must bear in mind that our expectations of a theory to deal with these matters are different from Plato's. Modern philosophy thinks of these as semantic problems, concerned with the correct understanding of thoughts such as 'The sum of seven and five is eleven' or 'The man I can see over there is Theaetetus'; we are concerned with the ways in which reference to a given item may be secured by different expressions. If we expect a semantic theory, we shall probably think that the Block gives us no more help than the Aviary. Plato indeed says that we should consider thought processes in terms of speech that the soul conducts with itself, a fruitful line of inquiry which he takes further in the *Sophist*. But the distinctions deployed in the Block and the Aviary—unlike some of those made in the *Sophist*—do not belong to semantic theory, and there is no direct relation between semantic conceptions and processes mentioned in the models: There is no suggestion, for instance, that when I think 'The man I can see is Theaetetus', what I *mean* is 'My present perception of a man fits my memory of Theaetetus'. Rather, the idea is that the process of having the thought involves my fitting the perception to my memory. Plato tries to proceed by distinguishing perceptual and nonperceptual ways of grasping, or getting at, an item—a distinction which, disastrously, has no analogue when we get to the Aviary.

How exactly the distinction between 'ways of grasping' is supposed to help with the problems, and how exactly it relates to what would now be discussed as semantic problems of reference, are questions that deserve careful consideration. We need to ask, too, why Plato is so concerned here with questions of mistaken identity. A simple answer is that this is the puzzle he has chosen to discuss here, a puzzle expressed in terms of taking one thing for another; later, in the *Sophist*, he will turn to descriptive falsehood, such as that involved in saying that Theaetetus is flying when he is in fact sitting. But Plato's concentration in the *Theaetetus* on identity mistakes does not come only from the puzzle he happens to have set himself. It relates, rather, to a radical discovery which Plato had made, and which resonates through the later part of the *Theaetetus* and in the *Sophist*: that *knowledge is necessary for error*.

In his earlier work, Plato had tended to assimilate error to ignorance. Ignorance, not knowing about something, can be seen as simply the negation of knowledge. In the case of expertise or a skill, ignorance is, basically, a void, the lack of the appropriate knowledge; equally, with ignorance of particular items, not to know of something is to have no thought about it. The *Republic*, in particular, in its dealings with knowledge, is overwhelmingly concerned with two topics, the kinds of skill that distinguish the rulers from the other classes in the city, and the distinctive subject matters to which various states of mind, and various studies, such as philosophy and mathematics, are addressed. Neither of these concerns is well designed to bring out distinctions between ignorance and error. The *Theaetetus* and the *Sophist*, on the other hand, address the fundamental point that error is not only different from mere ignorance, but, in a certain way, excludes it. I can make a mistake about something only if I know it, or know something about it, or know enough about it for my false belief to be a belief *about that thing*. These requirements could only seem very puzzling, until Plato took the first steps towards making them clear. Those steps required him to ask what it was that one needed to know in order to be in a position to make a mistake, and this naturally led first to problems about misidentification.

This concentration carries over into Part III, where the proposal is taken up that knowledge may be true belief together with a *logos*—an 'account', as we may best translate this very versatile word. Part III is the most compressed, and in some ways the most problematical, part of the dialogue, and the first problem which has to be faced is that it never discusses what, as we may be inclined to think, it should be discussing. The proposal in terms of an 'account' immediately follows the example of the jury, which straightforwardly refutes, as we saw earlier, the conception of knowledge as merely true judgement. Knowledge and true judgement cannot be the same thing, says Socrates (201c). 'That's just what I once heard a man say,' Theaetetus replies, 'he said that true judgement with an account is knowledge.' After this, we would expect the dialogue to pursue the kind of 'account' that could have turned the jurors' true belief into knowledge—their being able to offer a more reliable basis of such a belief, perhaps, such as that available to an eye-witness, or their being able to rehearse the details in a consistent way and to give good explanations in the face of objections (such considerations had indeed put in an appearance in a much earlier dialogue, the *Meno*). But nothing of this sort follows: The 'man's' proposal is elaborated in terms of a 'dream' recounted by Socrates, of a very abstract theory which seeks to construct knowable complexes from unknowable elements. The jury example serves as a transition to a discussion which does not pursue such examples, but rather reverts to a more basic level and seeks a better understanding of what it is to know a certain thing, to have a grasp of it. This contributes in itself to finding out what knowledge is, but it also has a broader theoretical relation to the puzzling conclusion which has emerged, that error presupposes knowledge.

The Dream has been much discussed, and scholars are not entirely agreed on the extent to which it refers to the theories of any specific thinker, as well as differing about its exact interpretation. More generally, critics have been puzzled by the extremely unspecific nature of the model: We are told nothing about the kinds of elements or wholes involved. However, the lesson to be drawn from the discussion is perhaps so general that it does not matter what the unspecified elements might be. The lesson is that there is going to be a systematic difficulty with any proposal to the effect that knowledge of a certain item should be explained in terms of an analysis into *unknowable* elements (202e). Exploiting some claims—seemingly very dubious—about the relations between notions such as 'whole', 'sum', and 'totality', Socrates is able to argue that either the complex is a knowable whole which must have knowable parts, or, alternatively, if the supposed parts or elements really are unknowable, then they cannot be *parts* of a complex at all. These arguments may seem specious, but once more we must bear in mind what they are supposed to do. Relations of part and whole puzzled Plato, as they did other Greek thinkers, but here he is undoubtedly clear that there is a difference between the complex or 'syllable', S-followed-by-O, and the mere pair of items, S and O. He is also aware that you can spell the syllable SO, but you cannot spell the letter S. His point, rather, is that spelling cannot be an adequate analogy to knowing: However exactly wholes are constructed of parts, knowable wholes cannot be constructed of unknowable parts. We must remember all the time the challenging requirement which has now emerged, that one must know a thing if one is to have a true or false belief about it. It follows from this that each of a set of letters (or any other such elements) will have to be known, if one is to believe of it that, together with the others, it forms a given complex; but, according to the Dream's account, this is exactly what someone will have to believe of each element, if he is to know the complex.

After rejecting the theory of the Dream, Socrates turns back to consider, more generally, what 'an account' might be. He lays aside the sense in which it means 'an expression of thought', for the obvious reason that true belief itself can receive such an expression—this cannot be what turns belief into knowledge. Two further candidates each raise, in turn, a very general difficulty of principle. One goes back to the sort of idea offered in the Dream, that an 'account' of a whole is to be given by listing its parts, and raises another problem, independent of the special point (about the parts being themselves unknowable) which has already been made against the Dream. If someone gives a correct enumeration of parts, we can always raise the question whether he knew that this was a correct enumeration of them, or whether (for instance) he got it right by luck. So we shall have to say that knowing a thing, or what a thing is, involves having a correct conception of it and *knowing* its composition in terms of its parts; and this gets us no further with an account of knowledge. If, last of all, it is proposed that the 'account' of a particular thing which will give us knowledge of it is to be found in a grasp of its distinguishing characteristics, of what marks it off from other things, we run into a difficulty very directly related to those raised by the Block and the Aviary: unless one grasps a thing's distinguishing characteristics, so that one can tell it from other things, one cannot even think of it, and so cannot get as far as having any conception of it at all, even one that falls short of knowledge.

The arguments of Part III make no secret of the fact that they leave much to be discussed. But the third Part is like the second, which more explicitly spells out its difficulties, and also like the first, which extensively deploys a complex argument, to the extent that they all belie the formally negative conclusion of the dialogue. We do not know at the end of it what knowledge is, but we understand better than we did at the beginning what might be involved in knowing what knowledge is. Thanks to a discussion which, even by Plato's standards, is exceptionally rich, inventive, and profound, we have been alerted to basic and very general problems not only in understanding knowledge, but in grasping what true or false belief might be, and what it is to think about a particular thing, whether correctly or incorrectly.

Plato says in the *Republic* that the dialectician, the person who pursues philosophy, is one who 'sees things together'. The *Theaetetus*, though it is one of the most analytical of Plato's dialogues and also, superficially, one of the more discontinuous in its argument, has a remarkable power to help us to do just that.

BRIEF BIBLIOGRAPHY

The major commentaries on the *Theaetetus* are all in English. The revised version of M. J. Levett's translation included in this volume was first published, together with a more extensive introduction, in

Myles Burnyeat, *The Theaetetus of Plato* (Indianapolis: 1990).

A commentary on the Greek text will be found in

Lewis Campbell, *The Theaetetus of Plato*, with a revised text and English notes, 2nd edition (Oxford: 1883).

The following are commentaries on other English translations, which the reader may find it useful to compare with Miss Levett's.

Francis Macdonald Cornford, *Plato's Theory of Knowledge*. The *Theaetetus* and the *Sophist* of Plato translated with a commentary (London: 1935).

John McDowell, *Plato: Theaetetus*. Translated with notes (Oxford: 1973).

A study of the dialogue without translation is

David Bostock, *Plato's Theaetetus* (Oxford: 1988).

More general books on Plato that contain substantial discussions of the *Theaetetus* include

W. G. Runciman, *Plato's Later Epistemology* (Cambridge: 1962).
Kenneth M. Sayre, *Plato's Analytic Method* (Chicago & London: 1969).
Nicholas P. White, *Plato on Knowledge and Reality* (Indianapolis: 1976).

There are many articles that throw light on particular aspects of the dialogues. The reader who wants to take the discussion further should consult the helpful list given by Myles Burnyeat in *The Theaetetus of Plato*, pages 243–48.

THE THEAETETUS OF PLATO: ANALYSIS

by M. J. Levett

[*Note*: The dialogue is a discussion of the question 'What is knowledge?' As in most of Plato's dialogues, the chief speaker is Socrates, who proceeds by eliciting from his companion a number of suggested definitions of knowledge. These are carefully examined, and in every case shown to be ultimately untenable. The conclusion of the dialogue is negative, and the whole effect may seem to be merely destructive. There is no doubt, however, that the discussion has not merely cleared the way for a more successful attempt, by ruling out a number of apparent possibilities, but has also pointed out the lines upon which further attempts may proceed. A considerable amount of positive teaching is concealed under the negative and destructive form.

References are to the pages and columns of the standard edition, given in the margin of most translations.]

of all things; of the things which are, that they are, and of the things which are not, that they are not.'

(ii) 152c–153d. Corresponding metaphysical theory of Heraclitus; nothing ever is, but everything is coming-to-be.

(iii) 153d–157d. Application of the theory of Heraclitus to the explanation of sense-perception.

(iv) 157e–160e. Application of these theories in explanation of delusions, dreams and the relativity of sense-perception.

(b) 160e–168c. *Superficial objections stated and answered.*

(i) 161c–161e. The theory seems to deny that there are differences of wisdom; why then was Protagoras himself thought to be specially wise? ANSWER (162d–163a): This proves nothing, and is a mere appeal to popular prejudice.

(ii) 163a–165e. The theory leads to the conclusion that we sometimes know and don't know at the same time, which is self-contradictory. ANSWER (166a–168c): All these contradictions disappear if we take seriously the infinite diversity and changeability of the world and of men's perceptions of it. Moreover (166d), when we take this seriously, we see that the theory need not deny that one man is wiser than another: it explains this by saying that one man is able to change the appearances and make them (not *true* instead of false, but) better instead of worse, while another has not this ability.

(c) 170a–172c, 177c–179b. *Serious refutation of Protagoras.*

(i) 170a–171d. The theory contradicts itself; for, since it holds that all opinions are equally true, it must admit the truth of the opinion that it (the theory itself) is false.

(ii) 171d–172c, 177c–179b. Grant that there are some cases, viz. matters of direct experience and of value, where, as the theory maintains, things are for the individual as they seem to him to be: *nevertheless* in certain other cases, viz. those involving judgements about the future, a man has not necessarily got the criterion in himself; one judgement may be true and another false, and one man wiser than another in the sense of 'better able to predict what is going to happen'.

(172c–177c. INTERLUDE: Character of the philosopher compared with that of the practical man.)

(d) 179c–183c. *Serious refutation of Heraclitus.*

(i) 179c–181b. General account of the Heracliteans, contrasted with the followers of Parmenides—the Monists.

(ii) 181b–183c. If it were true that everything is always changing in every way, it would be impossible to say or think anything at all. (And so the theory itself would be impossible.)

(e) 183c–186e. *Final refutation of the theory that knowledge is sense-perception* ('the Theory of Theaetetus').

(i) 184b–185a. Sense-perception depends on the bodily sense-organs—for example, the perception of colour on the eyes, of sounds on the ears; and the eye does not hear nor the ear see, i.e. each sense is confined to its proper objects.

(ii) 185a–e. But there are some properties, for example, being and not-being, likeness and unlikeness, same and different, which are common to the objects of all the senses. These must be considered by the soul functioning through itself without the aid of any special instrument.

(iii) 186a–e. These properties, including being and truth, are what we have to know if we are to have knowledge. Therefore, since these properties are not perceived through the senses, KNOWLEDGE IS NOT SENSE-PERCEPTION.

187a–201c. THIRD ATTEMPT TO DEFINE KNOWLEDGE: KNOWLEDGE IS TRUE JUDGMENT.

187a–c. Judgement, 'the activity of the soul when it is busy by itself about the things which are', may be either true or false. True judgement is to be knowledge. But what is false judgement?

(a) 187e–200d. *False judgement.*

(i) 188a–191a. The problem: It seems impossible to understand how there can be false judgements if

(1) (188a–c) everything is either something that we know or something that we do not know; or if

(2) (188c–189b) judging falsely is affirming the things which are not; or if

(3) (189b–191a) false judgement is judging that one thing is another.

(ii) 191a–200d. Attempts to explain false judgement by distinguishing different senses of the word 'know'.

(1) 191c–196c. *Simile of the Wax Block:* Memory distinguished from perception. False judgement can occur when you think (a) that other things you know and are perceiving are things you know, (b) that things you don't know but are perceiving are things you know, (c) that things you both know and are perceiving are other things you both know and are perceiving; and not otherwise. BUT (195b) mistakes *can* also occur in cases where perception is not concerned.

(196d–197a. *Note:* In order to carry on the discussion at all we have to make use of the very term, 'knowledge', which we are trying to define.)

(2) 197b 200d. *Simile of the Aviary:* the 'possession' of knowledge distinguished from the 'having' (application) of knowledge. False judgement is possible when you fail to 'have' (apply) knowledge which you possess. But (199c) this still does not account for our mistaking for knowledge something which is not knowledge.

(b) 200d–201c. *True judgement* is not the same thing as knowledge. For a good orator may persuade a jury to judge correctly about things which only an eye-witness could *know*.

201c–210a. FOURTH ATTEMPT TO DEFINE KNOWLEDGE. KNOWLEDGE IS TRUE JUDGEMENT ACCOMPANIED BY AN 'ACCOUNT'.

(a) 201d–202d. *Exposition:* There are elements, which cannot be known but only named; and compounds, which can be known if the names of the elements of which they are compounded are woven together into an account.

(b) 202d–206b. *Criticism:* Does the theory mean that a syllable, for example, can be known, but not its letters? Then

(i) (203c) if the syllable *is* the letters, the letters must be known if the syllable is. But

(ii) (203e) if the syllable is not the letters but some single form resulting from the combination of the letters, the syllable itself must be just as unknowable as the letters.

(iii) Further (206a), as a matter of common experience elements are more easily learnt, more 'knowable', than compounds.

(c) 206c–210a. *What then can be meant by 'account'?*

(i) 206d–e. Not the expression of thought in words, for then everyone who can express a judgement in words would have knowledge.

(ii) 206e–208b. Not a list of the elements of which the thing we are judging about is composed, for a man might be able to give such a list in one case although in another he might make mistakes about the very same elements; such a man could not be said to have knowledge even in the case where his judgement is correct.

(iii) 208c–210a. Not a grasp of the *difference* between one thing and another; for (209a–d) without such a grasp of the difference there would not even be correct judgement (so that it is not something which could be *added* to true judgement to make it into knowledge); and (209d–210a) to say we *know* the difference is to assume we understand the thing we are trying to define. 210b–d. *Conclusion:* None of the attempts to define knowledge succeeds.

Theaetetus

THEAETETUS

PERSONS OF THE DIALOGUE:
EUCLEIDES, TERPSION, SOCRATES, THEODORUS, AND THEAETETUS.

The prologue is supposed to take place in a street in Megara, and afterwards at the house of Eucleides, in the year 369 B.C. Eucleides and Terpsion are mentioned in Plato's Phaedo *(59c) as having come from Megara to keep company with Socrates on the day of his death. Little is known about them beyond the fact that Eucleides adhered to a strong version of the Socratic thesis that all the virtues are one thing, knowledge. He is thus a likely person to be interested in a Socratic discussion about knowledge.*

EUCLEIDES. TERPSION.

Eu. Are you only just in from the country, Terpsion? Or have you been here some time?

142

Ter. I've been here a good while. In fact, I have been looking for you in the market-place and wondering that I couldn't find you.

Eu. Well, you couldn't, because I was not in the city.

Ter. Where have you been, then?

Eu. I went down to the harbour; and as I was going, I met Theaetetus, being taken to Athens from the camp at Corinth.

Ter. Alive or dead?

Eu. Alive; but that's about all one could say. Badly wounded for one thing; but the real trouble is this sickness that has broken out in the army.

b

Ter. Dysentery?

Eu. Yes.

Ter. What a man to lose!

Eu. Yes. A fine man, Terpsion. Only just now I was listening to some people singing his praises for the way he behaved in the battle.

Ter. Well, there's nothing extraordinary about that. Much more to be wondered at if he hadn't distinguished himself. But why didn't he put up here at Megara?

c

Eu. He was in a hurry to get home. I kept asking him myself, and advising him; but he wouldn't. So I saw him on his way. And

1

as I was coming back, I thought of Socrates and what a remarkably good prophet he was—as usual—about Theaetetus. It was not long before his death, if I remember rightly, that he came across Theaetetus, who was a boy at the time. Socrates met him and had a talk with him, and was very much struck with his natural ability; and when I went to Athens, he repeated to me the discussion they

d   had had, which was well worth listening to. And he said to me then that we should inevitably hear more of Theaetetus, if he lived to grow up.

TER. Well, he appears to have been right enough.—But what was this discussion? Could you tell it to me?

Eu. Good Lord, no. Not from memory, anyway. But I made

143   some notes of it at the time, as soon as I got home; then afterwards I recalled it at my leisure and wrote it out, and whenever I went to Athens, I used to ask Socrates about the points I couldn't remember, and correct my version when I got home. The result is that I have got pretty well the whole discussion in writing.

TER. Yes, of course. I have heard you say that before, and I have always been meaning to ask you to show it to me, though I have been so long about it. But is there any reason why we shouldn't go through it now? I want a rest, in any case, after my journey in from the country.

b   Eu. Well, I shouldn't mind sitting down either. I saw Theaetetus as far as Erineum. Come along. We will get the slave to read it to us while we rest.

TER. Right.

Eu. This is the book, Terpsion. You see, I have written it out like this: I have not made Socrates relate the conversation as he related it to me, but I represent him as speaking directly to the persons with whom he said he had this conversation. (These were, he told me, Theodorus the geometer and Theaetetus.) I wanted, in the

c   written version, to avoid the bother of having the bits of narrative in between the speeches—I mean, when Socrates, whenever he mentions his own part in the discussion, says 'And I maintained' or 'I said,' or, of the person answering, 'He agreed' or 'He would not admit this.' That is why I have made him talk directly to them and have left out these formulae.

TER. Well, that's quite in order, Eucleides.

Eu. Now, boy, let us have it.

The scene of the dialogue itself is a gymnasium or wrestling-school in Athens and the date shortly before the death of Socrates in 399 B.C. Theodorus is a distinguished mathematician from Cyrene in Libya. Theaetetus, his pupil and a future mathematician of even greater distinction, is about 16 years old.

SOCRATES. THEODORUS. THEAETETUS.

Soc. If Cyrene were first in my affections, Theodorus, I should   *d*
be asking you how things are there, and whether any of your young people are taking up geometry or any other branch of philosophy. But, as it is, I love Athens better than Cyrene, and so I'm more anxious to know which of our young men show signs of turning out well. That, of course, is what I am always trying to find out myself, as best I can; and I keep asking other people too—anyone round whom I see the young men are inclined to gather. Now you, of course, are very much sought after, and with good reason; your geometry alone entitles you to it, and that is not your only claim.   *e*
So if you have come across anyone worth mentioning, I should be glad to hear.

THEOD. Well, Socrates, I think you ought to be told, and I think I ought to tell you, about a remarkable boy I have met here, one of your fellow-countrymen. And if he were beautiful, I should be extremely nervous of speaking of him with enthusiasm, for fear I might be suspected of being in love with him. But as a matter of fact—if you'll excuse my saying such a thing—he is not beautiful at all, but is rather like you, snub-nosed, with eyes that stick out; though these features are not quite so pronounced in him. I speak without any qualms; and I assure you that among all the people I   *144*
have ever met—and I have got to know a good many in my time— I have never yet seen anyone so amazingly gifted. Along with a quickness beyond the capacity of most people, he has an unusually gentle temper; and, to crown it all, he is as manly a boy as any of his fellows. I never thought such a combination could exist; I don't see it arising elsewhere. People as acute and keen and retentive as he is are apt to be very unbalanced. They get swept along with a rush, like ships without ballast; what stands for courage in their   *b*
make-up is a kind of mad excitement; while, on the other hand, the steadier sort of people are apt to come to their studies with minds that are sluggish, somehow—freighted with a bad memory. But this boy approaches his studies in a smooth, sure, effective way, and with great good-temper; it reminds one of the quiet flow of a

stream of oil. The result is that it is astonishing to see how he gets through his work, at his age.

Soc. That is good news. And he is an Athenian—whose son is he?

THEOD. I have heard the name, but I don't remember it. But he
c is the middle one of this group coming towards us. He and his companions were greasing themselves outside just now; it looks as if they have finished and are coming in here. But look and see if you recognise him.

Soc. Yes, I know him. He's the son of Euphronius of Sunium— very much the kind of person, my friend, that you tell me his son is. A distinguished man in many ways; he left a considerable property too. But I don't know the boy's name.

d THEOD. His name, Socrates, is Theaetetus. As for the property, that, I think, has been made away with by trustees. All the same, he is wonderfully open-handed about money, Socrates.

Soc. A thorough-bred, evidently. I wish you would ask him to come and sit with us over here.

THEOD. All right. Theaetetus, come here beside Socrates.

Soc. Yes, come along, Theaetetus. I want to see for myself what sort of a face I have. Theodorus says I am like you. But look. If you
e and I had each had a lyre, and Theodorus had told us that they were both similarly tuned, should we have taken his word for it straight away? Or should we have tried to find out if he was speaking with any expert knowledge of music?

THEAET. Oh, we should have enquired into that.

Soc. And if we had found that he was a musician, we should have believed what he said; but if we found he had no such qualification, we should have put no faith in him.

THEAET. Yes, that's true.

Soc. And now, I suppose, if we are interested in this question of our faces being alike, we ought to consider whether he is speak-
145 ing with any knowledge of drawing or not?

THEAET. Yes, I should think so.

Soc. Then is Theodorus an artist?

THEAET. No, not so far as I know.

Soc. Nor a geometer, either?

THEAET. Oh, there's no doubt about his being that, Socrates.

Soc. And isn't he also a master of astronomy and arithmetic and music—of all that an educated man should know?

THEAET. Well, he seems to me to be.

Soc. Then if he asserts that there is some physical resemblance

between us—whether complimenting us or the reverse—one ought
not to pay much attention to him?

THEAET. No, perhaps not.

Soc. But supposing it were the soul of one of us that he was   *b*
praising? Suppose he said one of us was good and wise? Oughtn't
the one who heard that to be very anxious to examine the object of
such praise? And oughtn't the other to be very willing to show
himself off?

THEAET. Yes, certainly, Socrates.

Soc. Then, my dear Theaetetus, now is the time for you to show
yourself and for me to examine you. For although Theodorus often
gives me flattering testimonials for people, both Athenians and
foreigners, I assure you I have never before heard him praise anybody in the way he has just praised you.   *c*

THEAET. That's all very well, Socrates; but take care he wasn't
saying that for a joke.

Soc. That is not Theodorus' way. Now don't you try to get out
of what we have agreed upon with the pretence that our friend is
joking, or you may make it necessary for him to give his evidence—
since no charge of perjury is ever likely to be brought against him.
So have the pluck to stand by your agreement.

THEAET. All right, I must, then, if that's what you've decided.

Soc. Tell me now. You are learning some geometry from Theodorus, I expect?

THEAET. Yes, I am.

Soc. And some astronomy and music and arithmetic?   *d*

THEAET. Well, I'm very anxious to, anyway.

Soc. And so am I, my son—from Theodorus or from anyone
who seems to me to know about these things. But although I get
on with them pretty well in most ways, I have a small difficulty,
which I think ought to be investigated, with your help and that of
the rest of the company.—Now isn't it true that to learn is to become
wiser[1] about the thing one is learning?

THEAET. Yes, of course.

Soc. And what makes men wise, I take it, is wisdom?

THEAET. Yes.

1. The words 'wise' and 'wisdom' in the argument which begins here represent
the Greek *sophos* and *sophia*. While there are good reasons for retaining the conven-
tional rendering of these terms, it is something of a strain to say that learning
geometry is becoming wiser about it. The point of the argument will come across
more naturally in English if readers substitute in their mind the words 'expert' and
'expertise'. Cf. Introduction, p. 3, pp. 19–20.

e Soc. And is this in any way different from knowledge?

THEAET. What?

Soc. Wisdom. Isn't it the things which they know that men are wise about?

THEAET. Well, yes.

Soc. So knowledge and wisdom will be the same thing?

THEAET. Yes.

Soc. Now this is just where my difficulty comes in. I can't get a proper grasp of what on earth knowledge really is. Could we man-

146 age to put it into words? What do all of you say? Who'll speak first? Anyone who makes a mistake shall sit down and be Donkey, as the children say when they are playing ball; and anyone who comes through without a miss shall be King and make us answer any question he likes.—Well, why this silence? Theodorus, I hope my love of argument is not making me forget my manners—just be- cause I'm so anxious to start a discussion and get us all friendly and talkative together?

b THEOD. No, no, Socrates—that's the last thing one could call forgetting your manners. But do make one of the young people answer you. I am not used to this kind of discussion, and I'm too old to get into the way of it. But it would be suitable enough for them and they would profit more by it. For youth can always profit, that's true enough. So do go on; don't let Theaetetus off but ask him some more questions.

Soc. Well, Theaetetus, you hear what Theodorus says. You won't want to disobey him, I'm sure; and certainly a wise man

c shouldn't be disobeyed by his juniors in matters of this kind—it wouldn't be at all the proper thing. Now give me a good frank answer. What do you think knowledge is?

THEAET. Well, I ought to answer, Socrates, as you and Theodorus tell me to. In any case, you and he will put me right, if I make a mistake.

Soc. We certainly will, if we can.

THEAET. Then I think that the things Theodorus teaches are knowledge—I mean geometry and the subjects you enumerated

d just now. Then again there are the crafts such as cobbling, whether you take them together or separately. They must be knowledge, surely.

Soc. That is certainly a frank and indeed a generous answer, my dear lad. I asked you for one thing and you have given me many; I wanted something simple, and I have got a variety.

THEAET. And what does that mean, Socrates?

Soc. Nothing, I dare say. But I'll tell you what I think. When you talk about cobbling, you mean just knowledge of the making of shoes?

THEAET. Yes, that's all I mean by it.

Soc. And when you talk about carpentering, you mean simply   *e*
the knowledge of the making of wooden furniture?

THEAET. Yes, that's all I mean, again.

Soc. And in both cases what you are doing is to define what the knowledge is of?

THEAET. Yes.

Soc. But that is not what you were asked, Theaetetus. You were not asked to say what one may have knowledge of, or how many branches of knowledge there are. It was not with any idea of counting these up that the question was asked; we wanted to know what knowledge itself is.—Or am I talking nonsense?

THEAET. No, you are perfectly right.

Soc. Now you think about this. Supposing we were asked about   147
some commonplace, every-day thing; for example, what is clay? And supposing we were to answer, 'clay of the potters' and 'clay of the stovemakers' and 'clay of the brickmakers', wouldn't that be absurd of us?

THEAET. Well, perhaps it would.

Soc. Absurd to begin with, I suppose, to imagine that the person who asked the question would understand anything from our answer when we say 'clay', whether we add that it is dollmakers'   *b*
clay or any other craftsman's. Or do you think that anyone can understand the name of a thing when he doesn't know what the thing is?

THEAET. No, certainly not.

Soc. And so a man who does not know what knowledge is will not understand 'knowledge of shoes' either?

THEAET. No, he won't.

Soc. Then a man who is ignorant of what knowledge is will not understand what cobbling is, or any other craft?

THEAET. That is so.

Soc. So when the question raised is 'What is knowledge?', to reply by naming one of the crafts is an absurd answer; because it points out something that knowledge is of when this is not what   *c*
the question was about.

THEAET. So it seems.

Soc. Again, it goes no end of a long way round, in a case where, I take it, a short and commonplace answer is possible. In the question about clay, for example, it would presumably be possible to make the simple, commonplace statement that it is earth mixed with liquid, and let the question of whose clay it is take care of itself.

THEAET. That seems easier, Socrates, now you put it like that. But I believe you're asking just the sort of question that occurred
d to your namesake Socrates here[2] and myself, when we were having a discussion a little while ago.

Soc. And what was that, Theaetetus?

THEAET. Theodorus here was demonstrating to us with the aid of diagrams a point about powers.[3] He was showing us that the power of 3 square feet and the power of 5 square feet are not commensurable in length with the power of 1 square foot; and he went on in this way, taking each case in turn till he came to the power of 17 square feet; there for some reason he stopped. So the idea occurred to us that, since the powers were turning out to be unlimited in number, we might try to collect the powers in question
e under one term, which would apply to them all.

Soc. And did you find the kind of thing you wanted?

THEAET. I think we did. But I'd like you to see if it's all right.

Soc. Go on, then.

THEAET. We divided all numbers into two classes. Any number which can be produced by the multiplication of equal numbers, we

---

2. Socrates the Younger, one of the group of friends with whom Theaetetus entered at the beginning. In later life he was a member of Plato's Academy.

3. A mathematical term for squares. By contrast, at 148ab 'power' is given a new, specially defined use to denominate a species of line, viz. the incommensurable lines for which the boys wanted a general account. It may be useful to give a brief explanation of the mathematics of the passage.

Two lines are incommensurable if and only if they have no common measure; that is, no unit of length will measure both without remainder. Two squares are incommensurable *in length* if and only if their sides are incommensurable lines; the areas themselves may still be commensurable, i.e. both measurable by some unit of area, as is mentioned at 148b. When Theodorus showed for a series of powers (squares) that each is incommensurable in length with the one foot (unit) square, we can think of him as proving case by case the irrationality of $\sqrt{3}$, $\sqrt{5}$, . . . $\sqrt{17}$. But this was not how he thought of it himself. Greek mathematicians did not recognize irrational *numbers* but treated of irrational quantities as geometrical entities: in this instance, lines identified by the areas of the squares that can be constructed on them. Similarly, we can think of the boys' formula for power or square lines at 148ab as making the point that, for any positive integer n, $\sqrt{n}$ is irrational if and only if there is no positive integer m such that $n = m \times m$. But, once again, a Greek mathematician would think of this generalization in the geometrical terms in which Theaetetus expounds it.

compared to a square in shape, and we called this a square or equilateral number.

Soc. Good, so far.

THEAET. Then we took the intermediate numbers, such as three and five and any number which can't be produced by multiplication of equals but only by multiplying together a greater and a less; a number such that it is always contained by a greater and a less side. A number of this kind we compared to an oblong figure, and called it an oblong number.

148

Soc. That's excellent. But how did you go on?

THEAET. We defined under the term 'length' any line which produces in square an equilateral plane number; while any line which produces in square an oblong number we defined under the term 'power', for the reason that, although it is incommensurable with the former in length, the plane figures which they respectively have the power to produce are commensurable. And there is another distinction of the same sort with regard to solids.

b

Soc. Excellent, my boys. I don't think Theodorus is likely to be had up for false witness.

THEAET. And yet, Socrates, I shouldn't be able to answer your question about knowledge in the same way that I answered the one about lengths and powers—though you seem to me to be looking for something of the same sort. So Theodorus turns out a false witness after all.

Soc. Well, but suppose now it was your running he had praised; suppose he had said that he had never met anyone among the young people who was such a runner as you. And then suppose you were beaten by the champion runner in his prime— would you think Theodorus' praise had lost any of its truth?

c

THEAET. No, I shouldn't.

Soc. But do you think the discovery of what knowledge is is really what I was saying just now—a small thing? Don't you think that's a problem for the people at the top?

THEAET. Yes, rather, I do; and the very topmost of them.

Soc. Then do have confidence in yourself and try to believe that Theodorus knew what he was talking about. You must put your whole heart into what we are doing—in particular into this matter of getting a statement of what knowledge really is.

d

THEAET. If putting one's heart into it is all that is required, Socrates, the answer will come to light.

Soc. Go on, then. You gave us a good lead just now. Try to imitate your answer about the powers. There you brought together the many powers within a single form; now I want you in the same way to give one single account of the many branches of knowledge.

e   THEAET. But I assure you, Socrates, I have often tried to think this out, when I have heard reports of the questions you ask. But I can never persuade myself that anything I say will really do; and I never hear anyone else state the matter in the way that you require. And yet, again, you know, I can't even stop worrying about it.

SOC. Yes; those are the pains of labour, dear Theaetetus. It is because you are not barren but pregnant.

THEAET. I don't know about that, Socrates. I'm only telling you what's happened to me.

149   SOC. Then do you mean to say you've never heard about my being the son of a good hefty midwife, Phaenarete?[4]

THEAET. Oh, yes, I've heard that before.

SOC. And haven't you ever been told that I practise the same art myself?

THEAET. No, I certainly haven't.

SOC. But I do, believe me. Only don't give me away to the rest of the world, will you? You see, my friend, it is a secret that I have this art. That is not one of the things you hear people saying about me, because they don't know; but they do say that I am a very odd sort of person, always causing people to get into difficulties. You must have heard that, surely?

b   THEAET. Yes, I have.

SOC. And shall I tell you what is the explanation of that?

THEAET. Yes, please do.

SOC. Well, if you will just think of the general facts about the business of midwifery, you will see more easily what I mean. You know, I suppose, that women never practise as midwives while they are still conceiving and bearing children themselves. It is only those who are past child-bearing who take this up.

THEAET. Oh, yes.

SOC. They say it was Artemis who was responsible for this custom; it was because she, who undertook the patronage of child

c   birth, was herself childless. She didn't, it's true, entrust the duties of midwifery to barren women, because human nature is too weak to acquire skill where it has no experience. But she assigned the task to those who have become incapable of child-bearing through age—honouring their likeness to herself.

THEAET. Yes, naturally.

---

4. The name means 'She who brings virtue to light'.

Soc. And this too is very natural, isn't it?—or perhaps necessary? I mean that it is the midwives who can tell better than anyone else whether women are pregnant or not.

THEAET. Yes, of course.

Soc. And then it is the midwives who have the power to bring on the pains, and also, if they think fit, to relieve them; they do it   *d* by the use of simple drugs, and by singing incantations. In difficult cases, too, they can bring about the birth; or, if they consider it advisable, they can promote a miscarriage.

THEAET. Yes, that is so.

Soc. There's another thing too. Have you noticed this about them, that they are the cleverest of match-makers, because they are marvellously knowing about the kind of couples whose marriage will produce the best children?

THEAET. No, that is not at all familiar to me.

Soc. But they are far prouder of this, believe me, than of cutting the umbilical cord. Think now. There's an art which is concerned   *e* with the cultivation and harvesting of the crops. Now is it the same art which prescribes the best soil for planting or sowing a given crop? Or is it a different one?

THEAET. No, it is all the same art.

Soc. Then applying this to midwifery, will there be one art of the sowing and another of the harvesting?

THEAET. That doesn't seem likely, certainly.

Soc. No, it doesn't. But there is also an unlawful and unscientific   *150* practice of bringing men and women together, which we call pro-curing; and because of that the midwives—a most august body of women—are very reluctant to undertake even lawful match-making. They are afraid that if they practise this, they may be suspected of the other. And yet, I suppose, reliable matchmaking is a matter for no one but the true midwife.

THEAET. Apparently.

Soc. So the work of the midwives is a highly important one; but it is not so important as my own performance. And for this reason, that there is not in midwifery the further complication, that the patients are sometimes delivered of phantoms and sometimes of   *b* realities, and that the two are hard to distinguish. If there were, then the midwife's greatest and noblest function would be to distin-guish the true from the false offspring—don't you agree?

THEAET. Yes, I do.

Soc. Now my art of midwifery is just like theirs in most respects. The difference is that I attend men and not women, and that I watch

over the labour of their souls, not of their bodies. And the most
c   important thing about my art is the ability to apply all possible tests
to the offspring, to determine whether the young mind is being
delivered of a phantom, that is, an error, or a fertile truth. For one
thing which I have in common with the ordinary midwives is that
I myself am barren of wisdom. The common reproach against me
is that I am always asking questions of other people but never
express my own views about anything, because there is no wisdom
in me; and that is true enough. And the reason of it is this, that
God compels me to attend the travail of others, but has forbidden
me to procreate. So that I am not in any sense a wise man; I cannot
d   claim as the child of my own soul any discovery worth the name of
wisdom. But with those who associate with me it is different. At
first some of them may give the impression of being ignorant and
stupid; but as time goes on and our association continues, all whom
God permits are seen to make progress—a progress which is amaz-
ing both to other people and to themselves. And yet it is clear that
this is not due to anything they have learnt from me; it is that they
discover within themselves a multitude of beautiful things, which
they bring forth into the light. But it is I, with God's help, who
deliver them of this offspring. And a proof of this may be seen in
e   the many cases where people who did not realise this fact took all
the credit to themselves and thought that I was no good. They have
then proceeded to leave me sooner than they should, either of their
own accord or through the influence of others. And after they have
gone away from me they have resorted to harmful company, with
the result that what remained within them has miscarried; while
they have neglected the children I helped them to bring forth, and
lost them, because they set more value upon lies and phantoms
than upon the truth; finally they have been set down for ignorant
fools, both by themselves and by everybody else. One of these
151   people was Aristeides the son of Lysimachus;[5] and there have
been very many others. Sometimes they come back, wanting my
company again, and ready to move heaven and earth to get it.
When that happens, in some cases the divine sign that visits me
forbids me to associate with them; in others, it permits me, and
then they begin again to make progress.

5. Grandson of a famous Athenian statesman; his education is under discussion in
Plato's *Laches*, where his father Lysimachus is anxious that his son should make
more of a name for himself than Lysimachus has managed to do. Evidently this did
not happen.

There is another point also in which those who associate with me are like women in child-birth. They suffer the pains of labour, and are filled day and night with distress; indeed they suffer far more than women. And this pain my art is able to bring on, and also to allay.

Well, that's what happens to them; but at times, Theaetetus, I *b* come across people who do not seem to me somehow to be pregnant. Then I realise that they have no need of me, and with the best will in the world I undertake the business of match-making; and I think I am good enough—God willing—at guessing with whom they might profitably keep company. Many of them I have given away to Prodicus;[6] and a great number also to other wise and inspired persons.

Well, my dear lad, this has been a long yarn; but the reason was that I have a suspicion that you (as you think yourself) are pregnant and in labour. So I want you to come to me as to one who is both the son of a midwife and himself skilled in the art; and try to answer *c* the questions I shall ask you as well as you can. And when I examine what you say, I may perhaps think it is a phantom and not truth, and proceed to take it quietly from you and abandon it. Now if this happens, you mustn't get savage with me, like a mother over her first-born child. Do you know, people have often before now got into such a state with me as to be literally ready to bite when I take away some nonsense or other from them. They never believe that I am doing this in all good-will; they are so far from realising that no God can wish evil to man, and that even I don't do this kind of *d* thing out of malice, but because it is not permitted to me to accept a lie and put away truth.

So begin again, Theaetetus, and try to say what knowledge is. And don't on any account tell me that you can't. For if God is willing, and you play the man, you can.

THEAET. Well, Socrates, after such encouragement from *you*, it would hardly be decent for anyone not to try his hardest to say what he has in him. Very well then. It seems to me that a man who *e* knows something perceives what he knows, and the way it appears at present, at any rate, is that knowledge is simply perception.

SOC. There's a good straight answer, my son. That's the way to speak one's mind. But come now, let us look at this thing together, and see whether what we have here is really fertile or a mere wind-egg. You hold that knowledge is perception?

6. A famous Sophist who specialized in fine distinctions of meaning between closely related words. Plato usually refers to him with dismissive irony.

THEAET. Yes.

SOC. But look here, this is no ordinary account of knowledge you've come out with: it's what Protagoras used to maintain. He said the very same thing, only he put it in rather a different way. For he says, you know, that 'Man is the measure of all things: of the things which are, that they are, and of the things which are not, that they are not.' You have read this, of course?

THEAET. Yes, often.

SOC. Then you know that he puts it something like this, that as each thing appears to me, so it is for me, and as it appears to you, so it is for you—you and I each being a man?

THEAET. Yes, that is what he says.

SOC. Well, it is not likely that a wise man would talk nonsense. So let us follow him up. Now doesn't it sometimes happen that when the same wind is blowing, one of us feels cold and the other not? Or that one of us feels rather cold and the other very cold?

THEAET. That certainly does happen.

SOC. Well then, in that case are we going to say that the wind itself, by itself, is cold or not cold? Or shall we listen to Protagoras, and say it is cold for the one who feels cold, and for the other, not cold?

THEAET. It looks as if we must say that.

SOC. And this is how it appears to each of us?

THEAET. Yes.

SOC. But this expression 'it appears' means 'he perceives it'?

THEAET. Yes, it does.

SOC. The appearing of things, then, is the same as perception, in the case of hot and things like that. So it results, apparently, that things are for the individual such as he perceives them.

THEAET. Yes, that seems all right.

SOC. Perception, then, is always of what is, and unerring—as befits knowledge.

THEAET. So it appears.

SOC. But, I say, look here. Was Protagoras one of those omniscient people? Did he perhaps put this out as a riddle for the common crowd of us, while he revealed the *Truth*[7] as a secret doctrine to his own pupils?

THEAET. What do you mean by that, Socrates?

SOC. I'll tell you; and this, now, is certainly no ordinary theory— I mean the theory that there is nothing which in itself is just one

_____

7. This appears to have been the title of Protagoras' book. See 161c.

thing: nothing which you could rightly call anything or any kind of thing. If you call a thing large, it will reveal itself as small, and if you call it heavy, it is liable to appear as light, and so on with everything, because nothing is anything or any kind of thing. What is really true, is this: the things of which we naturally say that they 'are', are in process of coming to be, as the result of movement and   *e* change and blending with one another. We are wrong when we say they 'are', since nothing ever is, but everything is coming to be.

And as regards this point of view, let us take it as a fact that all the wise men of the past, with the exception of Parmenides, stand together. Let us take it that we find on this side Protagoras and Heraclitus and Empedocles; and also the masters of the two kinds of poetry, Epicharmus in comedy and Homer in tragedy.[8] For when Homer talked about 'Ocean, begetter of gods, and Tethys their mother', he made all things the offspring of flux and motion.—Or don't you think he meant that?

THEAET. Oh, I think he did.

Soc. And if anyone proceeded to dispute the field with an army   *153* like that—an army led by Homer—he could hardly help making a fool of himself, could he?

THEAET. It would not be an easy matter, Socrates.

Soc. It would not, Theaetetus. You see, there is good enough evidence for this theory that being (what passes for such) and becoming are a product of motion, while not-being and passing-away result from a state of rest. There is evidence for it in the fact that heat and fire, which presumably generates and controls everything else, is itself generated out of movement and friction— these being motions.—Or am I wrong in saying these are the original sources of fire?

THEAET. Oh no, they certainly are.   *b*

Soc. Moreover, the growth of living creatures depends upon these same sources?

THEAET. Yes, certainly.

Soc. And isn't it also true that bodily condition deteriorates with

8. For Protagoras and Heraclitus, see Introduction. Empedocles described a cosmic cycle in which things are constituted and dissolved by the coming together and separating of the four elements earth, air, fire, and water. Epicharmus made humorous use of the idea that everything is always changing by having a debtor claim he is not the same person as incurred the debt. Parmenides remains outside the chorus of agreement because he held that the only reality is one single, completely changeless thing (cf. 183e).

rest and idleness? While by exertion and motion it can be preserved for a long time?

THEAET. Yes.

Soc. And what about the condition of the soul? Isn't it by learning and study, which are motions, that the soul gains knowledge and is preserved[9] and becomes a better thing? Whereas in a state

c of rest, that is, when it will not study or learn, it not only fails to acquire knowledge but forgets what it has already learnt?

THEAET. That certainly is so.

Soc. And so we may say that the one thing, that is, motion, is beneficial to both body and soul, while the other has the opposite effect?

THEAET. Yes, that's what it looks like.

Soc. Yes, and I might go on to point out to you the effect of such conditions as still weather on land and calms on the sea. I might show you how these conditions rot and destroy things, while the opposite conditions make for preservation. And finally, to put the crown on my argument, I might bring in Homer's golden cord,[10] and maintain that he means by this simply the sun; and is here explain-

d ing that so long as the revolution continues and the sun is in motion, all things are and are preserved, both in heaven and earth, but that if all this should be 'bound fast', as it were, and come to a standstill, all things would be destroyed and, as the saying goes, the world would be turned upside down. Do you agree with this?

THEAET. Yes, Socrates, I think that is the meaning of the passage.

Soc. Then, my friend, you must understand our theory in this way. In the sphere of vision, to begin with, what you would naturally call a white colour is not itself a distinct entity, either outside your eyes or in your eyes. You must not assign it any particular

e place; for then, of course it would be standing at its post; it wouldn't be in process of becoming.

THEAET. But what do you mean?

Soc. Let us follow what we stated a moment ago, and posit that

---

9. There seems to be a pun intended in the Greek. The word here translated as passive, 'is preserved', might equally well be taken as middle, meaning 'preserves in memory' (for which it is the regular word), with 'knowledge' as its object. The former interpretation is suggested by the use of the same word above, of preserving physical fitness; the latter by the mention of 'forgetting' below. But for the soul, to 'remember' is to 'be preserved'.

10. *Iliad* VIII 17–27. Zeus boasts that if he pulled on a golden cord let down from heaven, he could haul up earth, sea and all, bind the cord fast round the peak of Mt. Olympus, and leave the lot dangling in mid-air.

there is nothing which is, in itself, one thing. According to this theory, black or white or any other colour will turn out to have come into being through the impact of the eye upon the appropriate motion; and what we naturally call a particular colour is neither that which impinges nor that which is impinged upon, but some- *154* thing which has come into being between the two, and which is private to the individual percipient.—Or would you be prepared to insist that every colour appears to a dog, or to any other animal, the same as it appears to you?

THEAET. No, I most certainly shouldn't.

Soc. Well, and do you even feel sure that anything appears to another human being the same as it appears to you? Wouldn't you be much more disposed to hold that it doesn't always appear the same even to yourself because you never remain the same as yourself?

THEAET. Yes, that seems to me nearer the truth than the other.

Soc. Well now, supposing such things as size or warmth or *b* whiteness really belonged to the object we measure ourselves against or touch, it would never be found that this object had become different simply by coming into contact with another thing and without any change in itself. On the other hand, if you suppose them to belong to what is measuring or touching, this again could never become different simply because something else had come into its neighborhood, or because something had happened to the first thing—nothing having happened to itself. As it is, you see, we may easily find ourselves forced into saying the most astonishing and ridiculous things, as Protagoras would point out or anyone who undertook to expound his views.

THEAET. What do you mean? What sort of ridiculous things?

Soc. Let me give you a simple example of what I mean, and you *c* will see the rest for yourself. Here are six dice. Put four beside them, and they are more, we say, than the four, that is, half as many again; but put twelve beside them, and we say they are less, that is, half the number. And there is no getting out of that—or do you think there is?

THEAET. No, I don't.

Soc. Well now, supposing Protagoras or anyone else were to ask you this question: 'Is it possible, Theaetetus, to become bigger or more in number in any other way than by being increased?' What is your answer to that? *d*

THEAET. Well, Socrates, if I answer what seems true in relation to the present question, I shall say 'No, it is not possible'; but if I

consider it in relation to the question that went before, then in order
to avoid contradicting myself, I say 'Yes, it is.'

Soc. That's a good answer, my friend, by Jove it is; you are
inspired. But, I think, if you answer 'Yes', it will be like that episode
in Euripides—the tongue will be safe from refutation but the mind
will not.[11]

THEAET. That's true.

Soc. Now if you and I were professional savants, who had already analysed all the contents of our minds, we should now spend
our superfluous time trying each other out; we should start a regular
e   Sophists' set-to, with a great clashing of argument on argument.
But, as it is, we are only plain men; and so our first aim will be to
look at our thoughts themselves in relation to themselves, and
see what they are—whether, in our opinion, they agree with one
another or are entirely at variance.

THEAET. That would certainly be my aim, anyway.

Soc. And mine. That being so, as we are not in any way pressed
for time, don't you think the thing to do is to reconsider this matter
155   quietly and patiently, in all seriousness 'analysing' ourselves, and
asking what are these apparitions within us?—And when we come
to review them, I suppose we may begin with the statement that
nothing can possibly become either greater or less, in bulk or in
number, so long as it is equal to itself. Isn't that so?

THEAET. Yes.

Soc. Secondly, we should say that a thing to which nothing is
added and from which nothing is taken away neither increases nor
diminishes but remains equal.

THEAET. Yes, certainly.

b   Soc. Thirdly, that it is impossible that a thing should ever be
what it was not before without having become and without any
process of becoming?

THEAET. Yes, I think so.

Soc. Now it seems to me that these three statements that we
have admitted are fighting one another in our souls when we speak
of the example of the dice; or when we say that, within the space
of a year, I (a full-grown man) without having been either increased
or diminished, am now bigger than you (who are only a boy) and,
later on, smaller—though I have lost nothing and it is only that you

11. The allusion is presumably to *Hippolytus* 1. 612, where Hippolytus excuses
himself from keeping an oath by saying 'The tongue has sworn but the mind is
unsworn.'

have grown. For this means that I am, at a later stage, what I was   c
not before, and that, too, without having become—for without
becoming it is not possible to have become, and without suffering
any loss in size I could never become less. And there are innumera-
ble other examples of the same thing if once we admit these. You
follow me, I take it, Theaetetus—I think you must be familiar with
this kind of puzzle.

THEAET. Oh yes, indeed, Socrates, I often wonder like mad what
these things can mean; sometimes when I'm looking at them I begin
to feel quite giddy.

Soc. I dare say you do, my dear boy. It seems that Theodorus   d
was not far from the truth when he guessed what kind of person
you are. For this is an experience which is characteristic of a philosopher, this wondering: this is where philosophy begins and nowhere
else. And the man who made Iris the child of Thaumas was perhaps
no bad genealogist[12]—But aren't you beginning to see now what is
the explanation of these puzzles, according to the theory which we
are attributing to Protagoras?

THEAET. I don't think I am, yet.

Soc. Then I dare say you will be grateful to me if I help you to   e
discover the veiled truth in the thought of a great man—or perhaps
I should say, of great men?

THEAET. Of course I shall be, Socrates, very grateful.

Soc. Then you have a look round, and see that none of the
uninitiated are listening to us—I mean the people who think that
nothing exists but what they can grasp with both hands; people
who refuse to admit that actions and processes and the invisible
world in general have any place in reality.

THEAET. They must be tough, hard fellows, Socrates.   156

Soc. They are, my son—very crude people. But these others,
whose mysteries I am going to tell you, are a much more subtle
type. These mysteries begin from the principle on which all that
we have just been saying also depends, namely, that everything is
really motion, and there is nothing but motion. Motion has two
forms, each an infinite multitude, but distinguished by their powers, the one being active and the other passive. And through the

12. Hesiod, *Theogony* 265. 'Thaumas' means wonder, while Iris, the messenger of
the gods, is the rainbow which passes between earth and heaven. As a purely visual
phenomenon (nothing more to it than you see at a given moment), the rainbow is
nicely chosen as the divinity to represent the philosophic impulse on behalf of the
theory that knowledge is perception; contrast the role of Eros in Plato's *Symposium*
(201e–204b).

intercourse and mutual friction of these two there comes to be an
b   offspring infinite in multitude but always twin births, on the one
hand what is perceived, on the other, the perception of it, the
perception in every case being generated together with what is
perceived and emerging along with it. For the perceptions we have
such names as sight, hearing, smelling, feeling cold and feeling
hot; also what are called pleasures and pains, desires and fears; and
there are others besides, a great number which have names, an
infinite number which have not. And on the other side there is the
race of things perceived, for each of these perceptions perceived
c   things born of the same parentage, for all kinds of visions all kinds
of colours, for all kinds of hearings all kinds of sounds; and so on,
for the other perceptions the other things perceived, that come to
be in kinship with them.

Now what does this tale really mean, from our point of view,
Theaetetus? How does it bear on what we were saying before? Do
you see?

THEAET. Not really, Socrates.

SOC. Look here, then, let us see if we can somehow round it off.
What it is trying to express, presumably, is this. All these things
are in motion, just as we say; and their motion is distinguished by
its swiftness or slowness. What is slow has its motion in one and
the same place, and in relation to the things in the immediate
d   neighbourhood; in this way it generates and the offspring are
swifter, as they move through space, and their motion takes the
form of spatial movement.

Thus the eye and some other thing—one of the things commensu-
rate with the eye—which has come into its neighbourhood, generate both whiteness and the perception which is by nature united
with it (things which would never have come to be if it had been
anything else that eye or object approached). In this event, motions
e   arise in the intervening space, sight from the side of the eye and
whiteness from the side of that which cooperates in the production
of the colour. The eye is filled with sight; at that moment it sees,
and there comes into being, not indeed sight, but a seeing eye;
while its partner in the process of producing colour is filled with
whiteness, and there comes into being not whiteness, but white, a
white stick or stone or whatever it is that happens to be coloured
this sort of colour.

This account of course may be generally applied; it applies to all
that we perceive, hard or hot or anything else. Of these we must

understand in the same way—as indeed we were saying before—
that no one of them *is* anything in itself; all things, of all kinds
whatsoever, are coming to be through association with one another,
as the result of motion. For even in the case of the active and passive
motions it is impossible, as they say, for thought, taking them
singly, to pin them down to being anything. There is no passive till
it meets the active, no active except in conjunction with the passive;
and what, in conjunction with one thing, is active, reveals itself as
passive when it falls in with something else.

And so, wherever you turn, there is nothing, as we said at the
outset, which in itself is just one thing; all things are coming into
being relatively to something. The verb 'to be' must be totally   *b*
abolished—though indeed we have been led by habit and ignorance into using it ourselves more than once, even in what we
have just been saying. That is wrong, these wise men tell us,
nor should we allow the use of such words as 'something', 'of
something', or 'mine', 'this' or 'that', or any other name that makes
things stand still. We ought, rather, to speak according to nature
and refer to things as 'becoming', 'being produced', 'passing
away', 'changing'; for if you speak in such a way as to make things
stand still, you will easily be refuted. And this applies in speaking
both of the individual case and of many aggregated together—
such an aggregate, I mean, as people call 'man' or 'stone', or to   *c*
which they give the names of the different animals and sorts of
thing.

—Well, Theaetetus, does this look to you a tempting meal and
could you take a bite of the delicious stuff?

THEAET. I really don't know, Socrates. I can't even quite see what
you're getting at—whether the things you are saying are what you
think yourself, or whether you are just trying me out.

Soc. You are forgetting, my friend. I don't know anything about
this kind of thing myself, and I don't claim any of it as my own. I
am barren of theories; my business is to attend you in your labour.
So I chant incantations over you and offer you little tit-bits from
each of the wise till I succeed in assisting you to bring your own   *d*
belief forth into the light. When it has been born, I shall consider
whether it is fertile or a wind-egg. But you must have courage and
patience; answer like a man whatever appears to you to be true
about the things I ask you.

THEAET. All right, go on with the questions.

Soc. Tell me again, then, whether you like the suggestion that good and beautiful and all the things we were just speaking of cannot be said to 'be' anything, but are always 'coming to be'.[13]

THEAET. Well, as far as I'm concerned, while I'm listening to your exposition of it, it seems to me an extraordinarily reasonable view; and I feel that the way you have set out the matter has got to be accepted.

e   Soc. In that case, we had better not pass over any point where our theory is still incomplete. What we have not yet discussed is the question of dreams, and of insanity and other diseases; also what is called mishearing or misseeing or other cases of misperceiving. You realise, I suppose, that it would be generally agreed that all these cases appear to provide a refutation of the theory we *158*   have just expounded. For in these conditions, we surely have false perceptions. Here it is far from being true that all things which appear to the individual also are. On the contrary, no one of the things which appear to him really is.

THEAET. That is perfectly true, Socrates.

Soc. Well then, my lad, what argument is left for the person who maintains that knowledge is perception and that what appears to any individual also is, for him to whom it appears to be?

THEAET. Well, Socrates, I hardly like to tell you that I don't know what to say, seeing I've just got into trouble with you for that. *b*   But I really shouldn't know how to dispute the suggestion that a madman believes what is false when he thinks he is God; or a dreamer when he imagines he has wings and is flying in his sleep.

Soc. But there's a point here which *is* a matter of dispute, especially as regards dreams and real life—don't you see?

THEAET. What do you mean?

Soc. There's a question you must often have heard people ask— the question what evidence we could offer if we were asked whether in the present instance, at this moment, we are asleep and dreaming *c*   all our thoughts, or awake and talking to each other in real life.

THEAET. Yes, Socrates, it certainly is difficult to find the proof we want here. The two states seem to correspond in all their characteristics. There is nothing to prevent us from thinking when we are asleep that we are having the very same discussion that we have

---

13. An alternative translation would be: 'the suggestion that nothing is, but rather becomes, good, beautiful or any of the things we were speaking of just now'. The point is the same either way, for it is clear from 153d–154b that 'Nothing is in itself white' and 'White is nothing in itself' are to be treated as two sides of the same coin. The same will apply when 'is' is replaced, as here, by 'comes to be'.

just had. And when we dream that we are telling the story of a dream, there is an extraordinary likeness between the two experiences.

Soc. You see, then, it is not difficult to find matter for dispute, when it is disputed even whether this is real life or a dream. Indeed   *d* we may say that, as our periods of sleeping and waking are of equal length, and as in each period the soul contends that the beliefs of the moment are pre-eminently true, the result is that for half our lives we assert the reality of the one set of objects, and for half that of the other set. And we make our assertions with equal conviction in both cases.

Theaet. That certainly is so.

Soc. And doesn't the same argument apply in the cases of disease and madness, except that the periods of time are not equal?

Theaet. Yes, that is so.

Soc. Well now, are we going to fix the limits of truth by the clock?

Theaet. That would be a very funny thing to do.   *e*

Soc. But can you produce some other clear indication to show which of these beliefs are true?

Theaet. I don't think I can.

Soc. Then you listen to me and I'll tell you the kind of thing that might be said by those people who propose it as a rule that whatever a man thinks at any time is the truth for him. I can imagine them putting their position by asking you this question: 'Now, Theaetetus, suppose you have something which is an entirely different thing from something else. Can it have in any respect the same powers as the other thing?' And observe, we are not to understand the question to refer to something which is the same in some respects while it is different in others, but to that which is wholly different.

Theaet. In that case, then, it is impossible that it should have   *159* anything the same, either as regards its powers or in any other respect, if it is a completely different thing.

Soc. And aren't we obliged to admit that such a thing is also unlike the other?

Theaet. Yes, I think so.

Soc. Now supposing a thing is coming to be like or unlike to something, whether to itself or to something else; are we to say that when it is growing like it is coming to be the same, and when it is growing unlike it is coming to be a different thing?

Theaet. Yes, that must be so.

Soc. Now weren't we saying, at an earlier stage, that there is a number—indeed an infinite number—of both active and passive factors?

THEAET. Yes.

Soc. Also this, that when a thing mixes now with one thing and now with another, it will not generate the same things each time but different things?

b   THEAET. Yes, certainly.

Soc. Well, now let us apply this same statement to you and me and things in general. Take, for example, Socrates ill and Socrates well. Shall we say Socrates in health is like or unlike Socrates in sickness?

THEAET. You mean the ill Socrates as a whole compared with the well Socrates as a whole?

Soc. You get my point excellently; that is just what I mean.

THEAET. Unlike, then, I suppose.

Soc. And different also, in so far as he is unlike?

THEAET. Yes, that follows.

c   Soc. Similarly, you would say, when he is asleep or in any of the conditions we enumerated just now?

THEAET. Yes, I should.

Soc. Then it must surely be true that, when any one of the naturally active factors finds Socrates well, it will be dealing with one me, and when it finds Socrates ill, with a different me?

THEAET. Yes, surely.

Soc. Then in these two events the combination of myself as passive and it as the active factor will generate different things?

THEAET. Of course.

Soc. Now if I drink wine when I am well, it appears to me pleasant and sweet?

d   THEAET. Yes.

Soc. Going by what we earlier agreed, that is so because the active and passive factors, moving simultaneously, generate both sweetness and a perception; on the passive side, the perception makes the tongue percipient, while on the side of the wine, sweetness moving about it makes it both be and appear sweet to the healthy tongue.

THEAET. That's certainly the sense of what we agreed to before.

Soc. But when the active factor finds Socrates ill, then, to begin with, it is not in strict truth the same man that it gets hold of, is it? Because here, as we saw, it has come upon an unlike.

THEAET. Yes.

Soc. Then this pair, Socrates ill and the draught of wine, gener-   *e*
ates, presumably, different things again: a perception of bitterness
in the region of the tongue, and bitterness coming to be and moving
in the region of the wine. And then the wine becomes, not bitterness, but bitter; and I become, not perception, but percipient.

Theaet. Yes, quite.

Soc. And I shall never again become *thus* percipient of anything
else. A perception of something else is another perception, and
makes another and a changed percipient. Nor again, in the case of   *160*
that which acts on me, will it ever, in conjunction with something
else, generate the same thing and itself become such as it now is.
From something else it will generate something else, and itself
become a changed thing.

Theaet. That is so.

Soc. Nor will I become such for myself or it such for itself.

Theaet. No.

Soc. But I must necessarily become percipient of something
when I become percipient; it is impossible to become percipient,
yet percipient of nothing. And it again, when it becomes sweet or   *b*
bitter or anything of that kind, must become so for somebody,
because it is impossible to become sweet and yet sweet for no one.

Theaet. Quite impossible.

Soc. It remains, then, that I and it, whether we are or whether
we become, are or become for each other. For our being is, by
Necessity's decree, tied to a partner; yet we are tied neither to any
other thing in the world nor to our respective selves. It remains,
then, that we are tied to each other. Hence, whether you apply the
term 'being' to a thing or the term 'becoming', you must always
use the words 'for somebody' or 'of something' or 'relatively to
something'. You must not speak of anything as in itself either being
or becoming, nor let anyone else use such expressions. That is the   *c*
meaning of the theory we have been expounding.

Theaet. Yes, that's certainly true, Socrates.

Soc. Then since that which acts on me is for me, and not for
anyone else, it is I who perceive it too, and nobody else?

Theaet. Undoubtedly.

Soc. Then my perception is true for me—because it is always a
perception of that being which is peculiarly mine; and I am judge,
as Protagoras said, of things that are, that they are, for me; and of
things that are not, that they are not.

Theaet. So it seems.

Soc. How then, if I am thus unerring and never stumble in my   *d* thought about what is—or what is coming to be—how can I fail to be a knower of the things of which I am perceiver?

THEAET. There is no way you could fail.

SOC. Then that was a grand idea of yours when you told us that knowledge is nothing more or less than perception. So we find the various theories coincide:[14] that of Homer and Heracleitus and all their tribe, that all things flow like streams; of Protagoras, wisest of men, that man is the measure of all things; and of
e   Theaetetus that, these things being so, knowledge proves to be perception. What about it, Theaetetus? Shall we say we have here your first-born child, the result of my midwifery? Or what would you say?

THEAET. Oh, there's no denying it, Socrates.

SOC. This, then, it appears, is what our efforts have at last brought forth—whatever it really is. And now that it has been born, we must perform the rite of running round the hearth[15] with it; we must make it in good earnest go the round of discussion. For we must take care that we don't overlook some defect in this thing that is entering into life; it may be something not worth bringing up, a
161   wind-egg, a falsehood. What do you say? Is it your opinion that your child ought in any case to be brought up and not exposed to die? Can you bear to see it found fault with, and not get into a rage if your first-born is stolen away from you?

THEOD. Theaetetus will put up with it, Socrates. He is not at all one to lose his temper. But tell me, in Heaven's name, in what way is it not as it should be?

SOC. You are the complete lover of discussion, Theodorus, and it is too good of you to think that I am a sort of bag of arguments, and can easily pick one out which will show you that this theory is
b   wrong. But you don't realise what is happening. The arguments never come from me; they always come from the person I am talking to. All that I know, such as it is, is how to take an argument from someone else—someone who *is* wise—and give it a fair reception. So, now, I propose to try to get our answer out of Theaetetus, not to make any contribution of my own.

14. Literally, 'have converged to the same thing'.

15. We have not much information about the ceremony here alluded to. The authorities agree (1) that it was distinct from the formal adoption by the father, (2) that it was connected with the naming of the child, (3) that the friends and relatives sent presents of shell-fish. The above passage suggests that the ceremony was some sort of symbolic test of the child's fitness to take its place in the life of the family.

THEOD. That's a better way of putting it, Socrates; do as you say.

SOC. Well then, Theodorus, do you know what astonishes me about your friend Protagoras?

THEOD. No—what is it?

SOC. Well, I was delighted with his general statement of the theory that a thing is for any individual what it seems to him to be; but I was astonished at the way he began. I was astonished that he did not state at the beginning of the *Truth* that 'Pig is the measure of all things' or 'Baboon' or some yet more out-of-the-way creature with the power of perception. That would have made a most imposing and disdainful opening. It would have made it clear to us at once that, while we were standing astounded at his wisdom as though he were God, he was in reality no better authority than a tadpole—let alone any other man.

Or what are we to say, Theodorus? If whatever the individual judges by means of perception is true for him; if no man can assess another's experience better than he, or can claim authority to examine another man's judgement and see if it be right or wrong; if, as we have repeatedly said, only the individual himself can judge of his own world, and what he judges is always true and correct: how could it ever be, my friend, that Protagoras was a wise man, so wise as to think himself fit to be the teacher of other men and worth large fees; while we, in comparison with him the ignorant ones, needed to go and sit at his feet—we who are ourselves each the measure of his own wisdom? Can we avoid the conclusion that Protagoras was just playing to the crowd when he said this? I say nothing about my own case and my art of midwifery and how silly we look. So too, I think, does the whole business of philosophical discussion. To examine and try to refute each other's appearances and judgements, when each person's are correct—this is surely an extremely tiresome piece of nonsense, if the *Truth* of Protagoras is true, and not merely an oracle speaking in jest from the impenetrable sanctuary of the book.

THEOD. Protagoras was my friend, Socrates, as you have just remarked. I could not consent to have him refuted through my admissions; and yet I should not be prepared to resist you against my own judgement. So take on Theaetetus again. He seemed to be following you very sympathetically just now.

SOC. Now, Theodorus, supposing you went to Sparta and were visiting the wrestling-schools. Would you think it right to sit and watch other men exercising naked—some of them not much to look

at—and refuse to strip yourself alongside of them, and take your
turn of letting people see what you look like?

THEOD. Why not, if I could persuade them to leave the choice to
me? Similarly I am hoping to persuade you to allow me to be a
spectator and not drag me into the arena now that I am grown stiff;
but to take on someone who is younger and more supple.

SOC. Well, Theodorus, what you like I'll not dislike, as the saying
c   goes. So we must again resort to our wise Theaetetus. Come,
Theaetetus. Think, to begin with, of what we have just been saying,
and tell me if you are not yourself astonished at suddenly finding
that you are the equal in wisdom of any man or even a god?—Or
do you think the Protagorean measure isn't meant to be applied to
gods as much as to men?

THEAET. I most certainly don't. And, to answer your question,
yes, I am very much astonished. When we were working out the
d   meaning of the principle that a thing is for each man what it seems
to him to be, it appeared to me a very sound one. But now, all in
a minute, it is quite the other way round.

SOC. Yes, because you are young, dear lad; and so you lend a
ready ear to mob-oratory and let it convince you. For Protagoras,
or anyone speaking on his behalf, will answer us like this: 'My good
people, young and old,' he will say, 'you sit here orating; you
e   drag in gods, whose existence or nonexistence I exclude from all
discussion, written or spoken;[16] you keep on saying whatever is
likely to be acceptable to the mob, telling them that it would be a
shocking thing if no man were wiser than any cow in a field; but of
proof or necessity not a word. You just rely on plausibility; though
if Theodorus or any other geometer were to do that in his branch
of science, it's a good-for-nothing geometer he would be. So you
and Theodorus had better consider whether, in matters of such
importance, you are going to accept arguments which are merely
163 persuasive or plausible.'

THEAET. You wouldn't say we had any business to do that, Socrates; and neither should we.

SOC. Then, it seems, you and Theodorus say our criticism should
take a different line?

THEAET. Yes, it certainly should.

---

16. A reference to a notorious declaration by Protagoras: 'Concerning gods I am
unable to know whether they exist or do not exist, or what they are like in form [or:
appearance]; for there are many hindrances to knowledge, the obscurity of the
subject and the brevity of human life'.

Soc. Here, then, is another way in which we might consider whether knowledge and perception are the same or different things—for that is the question which our argument has held in view throughout, isn't it? And it was for its sake that we have unearthed all this extraordinary stuff?

THEAET. Undoubtedly.

Soc. Well, now, are we going to agree that when we perceive   *b* things by seeing or hearing them, we always at the same time *know* them? Take, for example, the case of hearing people speaking a foreign language which we have not yet learned. Are we going to say that we do not hear the sound of their voices when they speak? Or that we both hear it and know what they are saying? Again, supposing we do not know our letters, are we going to insist that we do not see them when we look at them? Or shall we maintain that, if we see them, we know them?

THEAET. We shall say, Socrates, that we know just that in them which we see and hear. We both see and know the shape and the colour of the letters; and with the spoken words we both hear and know the rise and fall of the voice. But what schoolmasters and   *c* interpreters tell us about them, we don't perceive by seeing or hearing, and we don't know, either.

Soc. Very good indeed, Theaetetus; and it would not be right for me to stand in the way of your progress by raising objections to what you say. But look, there is another difficulty coming upon us. You must think now how we are going to fend it off.

THEAET. What kind of difficulty?

Soc. I mean something like this. Supposing you were asked, 'If   *d* a man has once come to know a certain thing, and continues to preserve the memory of it, is it possible that, at the moment when he remembers it, he doesn't know this thing that he is remembering?' But I am being long-winded, I'm afraid. What I am trying to ask is, 'Can a man who has learnt something not know it when he is remembering it?'

THEAET. How could that happen, Socrates? That would be a most extraordinary thing.

Soc. Then am I perhaps talking nonsense? But think now. You say that seeing is perceiving and sight is perception?

THEAET. Yes.

Soc. Then a man who has seen something has come to know   *e* that which he saw, according to the statement you made just now?

THEAET. Yes.

Soc. But you do say—don't you?— that there is such a thing as memory?

THEAET. Yes.

Soc. Memory of nothing? Or of something?

THEAET. Of something, surely.

Soc. That is to say, of things which one has learnt, that is, perceived—that kind of 'something'?

THEAET. Of course.

Soc. And what a man has once seen, he recalls, I take it, from time to time?

THEAET. He does.

Soc. Even if he shuts his eyes? Or does he forget it if he does this?

THEAET. That would be a strange thing to say, Socrates.

164   Soc. Yet it is what we must say, if we are to save our previous statement. Otherwise, it's all up with it.

THEAET. Yes, by Jove, I begin to have my suspicions too; but I don't quite see it yet. You explain.

Soc. This is why. According to us, the man who sees has acquired knowledge of what he sees, as sight, perception and knowledge are agreed to be the same thing.

THEAET. Yes, certainly.

Soc. But the man who sees and has acquired knowledge of the thing he saw, if he shuts his eyes remembers but does not see it. Isn't that so?

THEAET. Yes.

b   Soc. But to say 'He doesn't see' is to say 'He doesn't know', if 'sees' is 'knows'?

THEAET. True.

Soc. Then we have this result, that a man who has come to know something and still remembers it doesn't know it because he doesn't see it? And that's what we said would be a most extraordinary thing to happen.

THEAET. That's perfectly true.

Soc. Then apparently we get an impossible result when knowledge and perception are identified?

THEAET. It looks like it.

Soc. Then we have got to say that perception is one thing and knowledge another?

THEAET. Yes, I'm afraid so.

c   Soc. Then what is knowledge? We shall have to begin again at the beginning, it seems. And yet—whatever are we thinking about, Theaetetus?

THEAET. What do you mean?

SOC. We appear to be behaving like a base-born fighting-cock, jumping away off the theory, and crowing before we have the victory over it.

THEAET. How are we doing that?

SOC. We seem to have been adopting the methods of professional controversialists: we've made an agreement aimed at getting words to agree consistently; and we feel complacent now that we have defeated the theory by the use of a method of this kind. We profess to be philosophers, not champion controversialists; and we don't realise that we are doing just what those clever fellows do.

d

THEAET. I still don't quite see what you mean.

SOC. Well, I will try to explain what I have in mind here. We were enquiring into the possibility that a man should not know something that he has learnt and remembers. And we showed that a man who has seen something, and then shuts his eyes, remembers but does not see it; and that showed that he does not know the thing at the very time that he remembers it. We said that this was impossible. And so the tale of Protagoras comes to an untimely end; yours too, your tale about the identity of knowledge and perception.

THEAET. So it appears.

e

SOC. But I don't think this would have happened, my friend, if the father of the other tale were alive. He would find plenty of means of defending it. As things are, it is an orphan we are trampling in the mud. Not even the people Protagoras appointed its guardians are prepared to come to its rescue; for instance, Theodorus here. In the interests of justice, it seems that we shall have to come to the rescue ourselves.

THEOD. I think you must. It is not I, you know, Socrates, but Callias, the son of Hipponicus,[17] who is the guardian of Protagoras' relicts. As it happened, I very soon inclined away from abstract discussion to geometry. But I shall be very grateful if you can rescue the orphan.

165

17. A wealthy Athenian famous for his patronage of the Sophists: 'a man who has spent more money on Sophists than everyone else put together' (*Apology* 20a). The discussion of Plato's *Protagoras* is set in his house, where Protagoras and other visiting Sophists are staying.

Soc. Good, Theodorus. Now will you give your mind to this rescue work of mine—what little I can do? Because one might be driven into making even more alarming admissions than we have just made, if one paid as little attention to the words in which we express our assertions and denials as we are for the most part accustomed to doing. Shall I tell you how this might happen? Or shall I tell Theaetetus?

Theod. Tell us both, Socrates; but the younger had better answer. It will not be so undignified for him to get tripped up.

b

Soc. Well, then, here is the most alarming poser of all. It goes something like this, I think: 'Is it possible for a man who knows something not to know this thing which he knows?'

Theod. What are we going to answer now, Theaetetus?

Theaet. That it is impossible, I should think.

Soc. But it is not, if you are going to premise that seeing is knowing. For what are you going to do when some intrepid fellow has you 'trapped in the well-shaft', as they say, with a question that leaves you no way out: clapping his hand over one of your eyes, he asks you whether you see his cloak with the eye that is covered—how will you cope with that?

c

Theaet. I shall say that I don't see it with this one, but I do with the other.

Soc. So you both see and do not see the same thing at the same time?

Theaet. Well, yes, in that sort of way I do.

Soc. 'That's not the question I'm setting you,' he will say, 'I was not asking you in what way it happened. I was asking you "Does it happen that you don't know what you know?" You now appear to be seeing what you don't see; and you have actually admitted that seeing is knowing, and not to see is not to know. I leave you to draw your conclusion.'

d

Theaet. Well, I draw a conclusion that contradicts my original suppositions.

Soc. And that is the kind of thing that might have happened to you more than once, you wonderful fellow. It might have happened if someone had gone on asking you whether it was possible to know sometimes clearly and sometimes dimly; or to know near at hand and not from a distance; or to know the same thing both intensely and slightly. And there are a million other questions with which one of the mercenary skirmishers of debate might ambush you, once you had proposed that knowledge and perception are the same thing. He would lay into hearing and smelling and other

perceptions of that kind; and would keep on refuting you and not
let you go till you had been struck with wonder at his wisdom—
that 'answer to many prayers'—and had got yourself thoroughly
tied up by him. Then, when he had you tamed and bound, he would
set you free for a ransom—whatever price seemed appropriate to
the two of you.[18]

But perhaps you'll ask, what argument would Protagoras himself
bring to the help of his offspring. Shall we try to state it?

THEAET. Yes, surely.

SOC. Well, he will say all the things that we are saying in our
attempt to defend him; and then, I imagine, he will come to grips
with us, and in no respectful spirit either. I imagine him saying:
'This good Socrates here—what he did was to frighten a small boy
by asking him if it were possible that the same man should at once
remember and not know the same thing; and when the boy in his
fright answered "No," because he couldn't see what was coming,
then, according to Socrates, the laugh was against *me* in the argument. You are too easy-going, Socrates. The true position is this.
When you are examining any doctrine of mine by the method of
question and answer, if the person being questioned answers as I
myself would answer, and gets caught, then it is I who am refuted;
but if his answers are other than I should give, then it is he who is
put in the wrong.

'Now, to begin with, do you expect someone to grant you that a
man's present memory of something which he has experienced in
the past but is no longer experiencing is the same sort of experience
as he then had? That is very far from being true. Again, do you
suppose he will hesitate to admit that it is possible for the same
man to know and not know the same thing? Or—if he has misgiv-
ings about this—do you expect him to concede to you that the man,

e

166

b

18. At this point the mercenary skirmisher is revealed as Protagoras himself. To
begin with, the skirmisher was made to sound like the Sophists Euthydemus and
Dionysodorus who are satirized in Plato's *Euthydemus*: a pair of elderly rogues who
are described as fiendishly clever combatants in argumentative warfare (*Euthyd.*
272a), keen to demonstrate their skills and to teach them to all comers—for a price
(274ab, 304c). They specialize in 'questions which leave no way out' (276e) and are
shown wielding a battery of teasers about knowing and not knowing (275d ff., 293b
ff.). But a ransom which is fixed by agreement between captor and captive can only
be a reference to a well-known practice of Protagoras' own: 'Anyone who comes to
learn from me may either pay the fee I ask for or, if he prefers, go to a temple, state
on oath what he believes to be the worth of my instruction, and deposit that amount'
(*Protagoras* 328bc, giving Protagoras' answer to a question closely related to that of
Theaetetus 161de, about his entitlement to set himself up to teach others for a fee).

who is in process of becoming unlike, is the same as he was before the process began? Do you expect him even to speak of "the man" rather than of "the men", indeed of an infinite number of these men coming to be in succession, assuming this process of becoming

c   unlike? Not if we really must take every precaution against each other's verbal traps. Show a little more spirit, my good man,' he will say, 'and attack my actual statement itself, and refute it, if you can, by showing that each man's perceptions are not his own private events; or that, if they are his own private events, it does not follow that the thing which appears "becomes" or, if we may speak of being, "is" only for the man to whom it appears. You keep talking about pigs and baboons; you show the mentality of a pig[19] yourself, in the way you deal with my writings, and you persuade your

d   audience to follow your example. That is not the way to behave.
'I take my stand on the truth[20] being as I have written it. Each one of us is the measure both of what is and of what is not; but there are countless differences between men for just this very reason, that different things both are and appear to be to different subjects. I certainly do not deny the existence of both wisdom and wise men: far from it. But the man whom I call wise is the man who can change the appearances—the man who in any case where bad things both appear and are for one of us, works a change and makes good things appear and be for him.

'And I must beg you, this time, not to confine your attack to the

e   letter of my doctrine. I am now going to make its meaning clearer to you. For instance, I would remind you of what we were saying before, namely, that to the sick man the things he eats both appear and are bitter, while to the healthy man they both appear and are the opposite. Now what we have to do is not to make one of these

167 two wiser than the other—that is not even a possibility—nor is it our business to make accusations, calling the sick man ignorant for judging as he does, and the healthy man wise, because he judges differently. What we have to do is to make a change from the one to the other, because the other state is *better*. In education, too, what we have to do is to change a worse state into a better state; only whereas the doctor brings about the change by the use of

19. The Greek pig appears often to be the type not so much of greed or uncleanliness, as of general lack of culture and of the finer perceptions. One spoke proverbially of things which 'not every pig would realise'. His shortcomings are intellectual as much as social or moral.

20. One of several puns on the title of Protagoras' book *Truth*.

drugs, the professional teacher[21] does it by the use of words. What never happens is that a man who judges what is false is made to judge what is true. For it is impossible to judge what is not, or to judge anything other than what one is immediately experiencing; and what one is immediately experiencing is always true. This, in my opinion, is what really happens: when a man's soul is in a pernicious state, he judges things akin to it, but giving him a sound state of the soul causes him to think different things, things that are good. In the latter event, the things which appear to him are what some people, who are still at a primitive stage, call "true"; my position, however, is that the one kind are *better* than the others, but in no way *truer*.

'Nor, my dear Socrates, should I dream of suggesting that we might look for wisdom among frogs. I look for wisdom, as regards animal bodies, in doctors; as regards plant-life, in gardeners— for I am quite prepared to maintain that gardeners too, when they find a plant sickly, proceed by causing it to have good and healthy, that is, "true" perceptions, instead of bad ones. Similarly, the wise and efficient politician is the man who makes wholesome things seem just to a city instead of pernicious ones. Whatever in any city is regarded as just and admirable *is* just and admirable, in that city and for so long as that convention maintains itself; but the wise man replaces each pernicious convention by a wholesome one, making this both be and seem just. Similarly the professional teacher who is able to educate his pupils on these lines is a wise man, and is worth his large fees to them.

'In this way we are enabled to hold both that some men are wiser than others, and also that no man judges what is false. And you, too, whether you like it or not, must put up with being a "measure". For this is the line we must take if we are to save the theory.

'If you feel prepared to go back to the beginning, and make a case against this theory, let us hear your objections set out in a connected argument. Or, if you prefer the method of question and answer, do it that way; there is no reason to try to evade that method either, indeed an intelligent person might well prefer it to any other. Only I beg that you will observe this condition: do not be unjust in your questions. It is the height of unreasonableness that a person who professes to care for moral goodness should be consistently unjust in discussion. I mean by injustice, in this connection, the behavior of a man who does not take care to keep

---

21. Literally, 'the Sophist'.

controversy distinct from discussion; a man who forgets that in controversy he may play about and trip up his opponent as often as he can, but that in discussion he must be serious, he must keep on helping his opponent to his feet again, and point out to him only those of his slips which are due to himself or to the intellectual society which he has previously frequented. If you observe this distinction, those who associate with you will blame themselves for their confusion and their difficulties, not you. They will seek your company, and think of you as their friend; but they will loathe themselves, and seek refuge from themselves in philosophy, in the hope that they may thereby become different people and be rid for ever of the men that they once were. But if you follow the common practice and do the opposite, you will get the opposite results. Instead of philosophers, you will make your companions grow up to be the enemies of philosophy.

'So, if you take my advice, as I said before, you will sit down with us without ill will or hostility, in a kindly spirit. You will genuinely try to find out what our meaning is when we maintain (a) that all things are in motion and (b) that for each person and each city, things are what they seem to them to be. And upon this basis you will enquire whether knowledge and perception are the same thing or different things. But you will not proceed as you did just now. You will not base your argument upon the use and wont of language; you will not follow the practice of most men, who drag words this way and that at their pleasure, so making every imaginable difficulty for one another.'

Well, Theodorus, here is my contribution to the rescue of your friend—the best I can do, with my resources, and little enough that is. If he were alive himself, he would have come to the rescue of his offspring in a grander style.

THEOD. That must be a joke, Socrates. It was a very spirited rescue.

SOC. You are kind, my friend. Tell me now, did you notice that Protagoras was complaining of us, in the speech that we have just heard, for addressing our arguments to a small boy and making the child's nervousness a weapon against his ideas? And how he disparaged our method of argument as merely an amusing game, and how solemnly he upheld his 'measure of all things' and commanded us to be serious when we dealt with his theory?

THEOD. Yes, of course I noticed that, Socrates.

SOC. Then do you think we should obey his commands?

THEOD. Most certainly I do.

Soc. Look at the company then. They are all children but you. So if we are to obey Protagoras, it is you and I who have got to be serious about his theory. It is you and I who must question and answer one another. Then he will not have *this* against us, at any rate, that we turned the criticism of his philosophy into sport with boys.

e

THEOD. Well, isn't our Theaetetus better able to follow the investigation of a theory than many an old fellow with a long beard?

Soc. But not better than *you*, Theodorus. Do not go on imagining that it is my business to be straining every nerve to defend your dead friend while you do nothing. Come now, my very good Theodorus, come a little way with me. Come with me at any rate until we see whether in questions of geometrical proofs it is really you who should be the measure or whether all men are as sufficient to themselves as you are in astronomy and the other sciences in which you have made your name.

169

THEOD. Socrates, it is not easy for a man who has sat down beside you to refuse to talk. That was all nonsense just now when I was pretending that you were going to allow me to keep my coat on, and not use compulsion like the Spartans. So far from that, you seem to me to have leanings towards the methods of Sciron.[22] The Spartans tell one either to strip or to go away; but you seem rather to be playing the part of Antaeus.[23] You don't let any comer go till you have stripped him and made him wrestle with you in an argument.

b

Soc. That, Theodorus, is an excellent simile to describe what is the matter with me. But I am more of a fiend for exercise than Sciron and Antaeus. I have met with many and many a Heracles and Theseus in my time, mighty men of words; and they have well battered me. But for all that I don't retire from the field, so terrible a lust has come upon me for these exercises. *You* must not grudge me this, either; try a fall with me and we shall both be the better.

c

THEOD. All right. I resign myself; take me with you where you

22. A legendary highwayman who attacked travellers on the coast between Megara and Corinth. His most famous 'method' was to compel them to wash his feet, and kick them over the cliff into the sea while they were so doing. He was said to have been himself disposed of in a similar manner by Theseus.

23. Antaeus belongs to a tradition current among the Greek colonists of North Africa, and primarily connected with the neighbourhood of Cyrene. He was said to have lived in a cave and compelled all passers-by to wrestle with him, with results invariably fatal to them. He was finally put out of action by Heracles.

like. In any case, I see, I have got to put up with the fate you spin
for me, and submit to your inquisition. But not further than the
limits you have laid down; beyond that I shall not be able to offer
myself.

SOC. It will do if you will go with me so far. Now there is one
kind of mistake I want you to be specially on your guard against,
namely, that we do not unconsciously slip into some childish form
d of argument. We don't want to get into disgrace for this again.

THEOD. I will do my best, I promise you.

SOC. The first thing, then, is to tackle the same point that we
were dealing with before. We were making a complaint. Now let
us see whether we were right or wrong in holding it to be a defect
in this theory that it made every man self-sufficient in wisdom; and
whether we were right or wrong when we made Protagoras concede
that some men are superior to others in questions of better and
worse, these being 'the wise'. Do you agree?

THEOD. Yes.

SOC. It would be a different matter if Protagoras were here in
person and agreed with us, instead of our having made this conces-
e sion on his behalf in our attempt to help him. In that case, there
would be no need to take this question up again and make sure
about it. In the circumstances, however, it might be decided that
we had no authority on his behalf, and so it is desirable that we
should come to a clearer agreement on this point; for it makes no
small difference whether this is so or not.

THEOD. True.

SOC. Then don't let us obtain this concession through anybody
170 else. Let us take the shortest way, an appeal to his own statement.

THEOD. How?

SOC. In this way. He says, does he not, that things are for every
man what they seem to him to be?

THEOD. Yes, that is what he says.

SOC. Well, then, Protagoras, we too are expressing the judgements of a man—I might say, of all men—when we say that there
is no one in the world who doesn't believe that in some matters he
is wiser than other men; while in other matters, they are wiser than
he. In emergencies—if at no other time—you see this belief. When
they are in distress, on the battlefield, or in sickness or in a storm
at sea, all men turn to their leaders in each sphere as to God, and
b look to them for salvation because they are superior in precisely
this one thing—knowledge. And wherever human life and work
goes on, you find everywhere men seeking teachers and masters,

for themselves and for other living creatures and for the direction
of all human works. You find also men who believe that they are
able to teach[24] and to take the lead. In all these cases, what else can
we say but that men do believe in the existence of both wisdom
and ignorance among themselves?

THEOD. There can be no other conclusion.

Soc. And they believe that wisdom is true thinking? While ignorance is a matter of false judgement?

THEOD. Yes, of course.   c

Soc. What then, Protagoras, are we to make of your argument?
Are we to say that all men, on every occasion, judge what is true?
Or that they judge sometimes truly and sometimes falsely? Which-
ever we say, it comes to the same thing, namely, that men do not
always judge what is true; that human judgements are both true
and false. For think, Theodorus. Would you, would anyone of the
school of Protagoras be prepared to contend that no one ever thinks
his neighbour is ignorant or judging falsely?

THEOD. No, that's not a thing one could believe, Socrates.

Soc. And yet it is to this that our theory has been driven—this   d
theory that man is the measure of all things.

THEOD. How is that?

Soc. Well, suppose you come to a decision in your own mind
and then express a judgement about something to me. Let us assume with Protagoras that your judgement is true for *you*. But isn't
it possible that the rest of us may criticise your verdict? Do we
always agree that your judgement is true? Or does there rise up
against you, every time, a vast army of persons who think the
opposite, who hold that your decisions and your thoughts are false?

THEOD. Heaven knows they do, Socrates, in their 'thousands   e
and tens of thousands', as Homer says, and give me all the trouble
that is humanly possible.

Soc. Then do you want us to say that you are then judging what
is true for yourself, but false for the tens of thousands?

THEOD. It looks as if that is what we must say, according to the
theory, at any rate.

Soc. And what of Protagoras himself? Must he not say this, that
supposing he himself did not believe that man is the measure, any
more than the majority of people (who indeed do not believe it),
then this *Truth* which he wrote is true for no one? On the other
hand, suppose he believed it himself, but the majority of men do   *171*

24. Protagoras himself professed to teach 'virtue'.

not agree with him; then you see—to begin with—the more those to whom it does not seem to be the truth outnumber those to whom it does, so much the more it isn't than it is?

THEOD. That must be so, if it is going to be or not be according to the individual judgement.

Soc. Secondly, it has this most exquisite feature: Protagoras admits, I presume, that the contrary opinion about his own opinion (namely, that it is false) must be true, seeing he agrees that all men judge what is.

THEOD. Undoubtedly.

b Soc. And in conceding the truth of the opinion of those who think him wrong, he is really admitting the falsity of his own opinion?

THEOD. Yes, inevitably.

Soc. But for their part the others do not admit that they are wrong?

THEOD. No.

Soc. But Protagoras again admits *this* judgement to be true, according to his written doctrine?

THEOD. So it appears.

Soc. It will be disputed, then, by everyone, beginning with Protagoras—or rather, it will be admitted by him, when he grants to the person who contradicts him that he judges truly—when he

c does that, even Protagoras himself will be granting that neither a dog nor the 'man in the street' is the measure of anything at all which he has not learned. Isn't that so?

THEOD. It is so.

Soc. Then since it is disputed by everyone, the *Truth* of Protagoras is not true for anyone at all, not even for himself?

THEOD. Socrates, we are running my friend too hard.

Soc. But it is not at all clear, my dear Theodorus, that we are running off the right track. Hence it is likely that Protagoras, being older than we are, really is wiser as well;[25] and if he were to stick

d up his head from below as far as the neck just here where we are, he would in all likelihood convict me twenty times over of talking nonsense, and show you up too for agreeing with me, before he ducked down to rush off again. But we have got to take ourselves as we are, I suppose, and go on saying the things which seem to

25. Because the refutation of the thesis that everyone is equally wise establishes that some are wiser than others— and who should this be (Socrates suggests with savage irony) but Protagoras himself?

us to be. At the moment, then, mustn't we maintain that any man would admit at least this, that some men are wiser than their fellows and others more ignorant?

THEOD. So it seems to me, at any rate.

SOC. We may also suggest that the theory would stand firm most successfully in the position which we sketched out for it in our *e* attempt to bring help to Protagoras. I mean the position that most things are for the individual what they seem to him to be; for instance, warm, dry, sweet and all this type of thing. But if the theory is going to admit that there is any sphere in which one man is superior to another, it might perhaps be prepared to grant it in questions of what is good or bad for one's health. Here it might well be admitted that it is not true that every creature—woman or child or even animal—is competent to recognise what is good for it and to heal its own sickness; that here, if anywhere, one person is better than another. Do you agree?

THEOD. Yes, that seems so to me.

SOC. Then consider political questions. Some of these are ques- *172* tions of what may or may not fittingly be done, of just and unjust, of what is sanctioned by religion and what is not; and here the theory may be prepared to maintain that whatever view a city takes on these matters and establishes as its law or convention, is truth and fact for that city. In such matters neither any individual nor any city can claim superior wisdom. But when it is a question of laying down what is to the interest of the state and what is not, the matter is different. The theory will again admit that here, if anywhere, one counsellor is better than another; here the decision of one city may be more in conformity with the truth than that of another. It would certainly not have the hardihood to affirm that *b* when a city decides that a certain thing is to its own interest, that thing will undoubtedly turn out to be to its interest. It is in those other questions I am talking about—just and unjust, religious and irreligious—that men are ready to insist that no one of these things has by nature any being of its own; in respect of these, they say, what seems to people collectively to be so is true, at the time when it seems that way and for just as long as it so seems. And even those who are not prepared to go all the way with Protagoras take some such view of wisdom.[26] But I see, Theodorus, that we are becoming involved in a greater discussion emerging from the lesser one. *c*

26. On the translation of this and the preceding sentence, see Introduction, Part I, n. 41.

THEOD. Well, we have plenty of time, haven't we, Socrates?

SOC. We appear to . . . That remark of yours, my friend, reminds me of an idea that has often occurred to me before—how natural it is that men who have spent a great part of their lives in philosophical studies make such fools of themselves when they appear as speakers in the law-courts.

THEOD. How do you mean now?

SOC. Well, look at the man who has been knocking about in law-courts and such places ever since he was a boy; and compare him with the man brought up in philosophy, in the life of a student. It *d* is surely like comparing the up-bringing of a slave with that of a free man.

THEOD. How is that, now?

SOC. Because the one man always has what you mentioned just now—plenty of time. When he talks, he talks in peace and quiet, and his time is his own. It is so with us now: here we are beginning on our third new discussion;[27] and he can do the same, if he is like us, and prefers the new-comer to the question in hand. It does not matter to such men whether they talk for a day or a year, if only they may hit upon that which is. But the other—the man of the *e* law-courts—is always in a hurry when he is talking; he has to speak with one eye on the clock. Besides, he can't make his speeches on any subject he likes; he has his adversary standing over him, armed with compulsory powers and with the sworn statement, which is read out point by point as he proceeds, and must be kept to by the speaker. The talk is always about a fellow-slave, and is addressed to a master,[28] who sits there holding some suit or other in his hand. And the struggle is never a matter of indifference; it always directly concerns the speaker, and sometimes life itself is at stake.

173   Such conditions make him keen and highly-strung, skilled in flattering the master and working his way into favour; but cause his soul to be small and warped. His early servitude prevents him from making a free, straight growth; it forces him into doing crooked things by imposing dangers and alarms upon a soul that is still tender. He cannot meet these by just and honest practice, and so resorts to lies and to the policy of repaying one wrong with another;

27. If the 'greater discussion' emerging at 172c is the 'third', the other two are probably the two attempts to come to grips with Protagoras beginning respectively at 161b and 169d.

28. The master is the *dēmos*, the people, embodied in the jury of several hundred persons who decide the suit.

thus he is constantly being bent and distorted, and in the end grows   *b*
up to manhood with a mind that has no health in it, having now
become—in his own eyes—a man of ability and wisdom.
There is your practical man, Theodorus. What about our own
set? Would you like us to have a review of them, or shall we let
them be, and return to the argument? We don't want to abuse this
freedom to change our subject of which we were speaking just now.
THEOD. No, no, Socrates. Let us review the philosophers. What
you said just now was quite right; we who move in such circles are   *c*
not the servants but the masters of our discussions. Our arguments
are our own, like slaves; each one must wait about for us, to be
finished whenever we think fit. We have no jury, and no audience
(as the dramatic poets have), sitting in control over us, ready to
criticise and give orders.
SOC. Very well, then; we must review them, it seems, since you
have made up your mind. But let us confine ourselves to the leaders;
why bother about the second-rate specimens? To begin with, then,
the philosopher grows up without knowing the way to the market-
place, or the whereabouts of the law-courts or the council-chambers   *d*
or any other place of public assembly. Laws and decrees, published
orally or in writing, are things he never sees or hears. The scram-
bling of political cliques for office; social functions, dinners, parties
with flute-girls—such doings never enter his head even in a dream.
So with questions of birth—he has no more idea whether a fellow-
citizen is high-born or humble, or whether he has inherited some
taint from his forbears, male or female, than he has of the number
of pints in the sea, as they say. And in all these matters, he knows   *e*
not even that he knows not; for he does not hold himself aloof from
them in order to get a reputation, but because it is in reality only
his body that lives and sleeps in the city. His mind, having come
to the conclusion that all these things are of little or no account,
spurns them and pursues its wingéd way, as Pindar says, throughout the universe, 'in the deeps below the earth' and 'in the heights
above the heaven'; geometrising upon earth, measuring its sur-
faces, astronomising in the heavens; tracking down by every path
the entire nature of each whole among the things that are, and   *174*
never condescending to what lies near at hand.
THEOD. What do you mean by that, Socrates?
SOC. Well, here's an instance: they say Thales[29] was studying the

29. The first founder of Greek natural philosophy (sixth century B.C.), about whom
we have anecdotes but little solid information. Plato's anecdote of Thales falling into

stars, Theodorus, and gazing aloft, when he fell into a well; and a witty and amusing Thracian servant-girl made fun of him because, she said, he was wild to know about what was up in the sky but failed to see what was in front of him and under his feet. The same joke applies to all who spend their lives in philosophy. It really is

b true that the philosopher fails to see his next-door neighbour; he not only doesn't notice what he is doing; he scarcely knows whether he is a man or some other kind of creature. The question he asks is, What is Man? What actions and passions properly belong to human nature and distinguish it from all other beings? This is what he wants to know and concerns himself to investigate. You see what I mean, Theodorus, don't you?

THEOD. Yes; and what you say is true.

SOC. This accounts, my friend, for the behaviour of such a man when he comes into contact with his fellows, either privately with

c individuals or in public life, as I was saying at the beginning. Whenever he is obliged, in a law-court or elsewhere, to discuss the things that lie at his feet and before his eyes, he causes entertainment not only to Thracian servant-girls but to all the common herd, by tumbling into wells and every sort of difficulty through his lack of experience. His clumsiness is awful and gets him a reputation for fatuousness. On occasions when personal scandal is the topic of conversation, he never has anything at all of his own to contribute; he knows nothing to the detriment of anyone, never having paid any attention to this subject—a lack of resource which makes

d him look very comic. And again, when compliments are in order, and self-laudation, his evident amusement—which is by no means a pose but perfectly genuine—is regarded as idiotic. When he hears the praises of a despot or a king being sung, it sounds to his ears as if some stock-breeder were being congratulated—some keeper of pigs or sheep, or cows that are giving him plenty of milk; only he thinks that the rulers have a more difficult and treacherous animal to rear and milk, and that such a man, having no spare time,

e is bound to become quite as coarse and uncultivated as the stock-farmer; for the castle of the one is as much a prison as the mountain

---

a well is complemented or counterbalanced by one in Aristotle, *Politics* I 4, 1259a 6–19, which tells of Thales using his astronomical knowledge to predict a large olive crop, hiring all the available olive-presses while it was still winter, and then, when the season brought a great demand for presses, leasing them out at a large profit. The moral: it is easy for philosophers to be rich if they wish, but that is not what they are interested in. Anecdotes like these featured frequently in philosophical debates about the ideal form of life.

fold of the other. When he hears talk of land—that so-and-so has a property of ten thousand acres or more, and what a vast property that is, it sounds to him like a tiny plot, used as he is to envisage the whole earth. When his companions become lyric on the subject of great families, and exclaim at the noble blood of one who can point to seven wealthy ancestors, he thinks that such praise comes of a dim and limited vision, an inability, through lack of education, to take a steady view of the whole, and to calculate that every single *175* man has countless hosts of ancestors, near and remote, amongst whom are to be found, in every instance, rich men and beggars, kings and slaves, Greeks and foreigners, by the thousand. When men pride themselves upon a pedigree of twenty-five ancestors, and trace their descent back to Heracles the son of Amphitryon, they seem to him to be taking a curious interest in trifles. As for the twenty-fifth ancestor of Amphitryon, what *he* may have been is *b* merely a matter of luck, and similarly with the fiftieth before him again. How ridiculous, he thinks, not to be able to work that out, and get rid of the gaping vanity of a silly mind.

On all these occasions, you see, the philosopher is the object of general derision, partly for what men take to be his superior manner, and partly for his constant ignorance and lack of resource in dealing with the obvious.

THEOD. What you say exactly describes what does happen, Socrates.

Soc. But consider what happens, my friend, when he in his turn draws someone to a higher level, and induces him to abandon questions of 'My injustice towards you, or yours towards me' for an ex- *c* amination of justice and injustice themselves—what they are, and how they differ from everything else and from each other; or again, when he gets him to leave such questions as 'Is a king happy?' or 'a man of property?' for an enquiry into kingship, and into human happiness and misery in general—what these two things are, and what, for a human being, is the proper method by which the one can be obtained and the other avoided. When it is an account of matters like all these that is demanded of our friend with the small, *d* sharp, legal mind, the situation is reversed; his head swims as, suspended at such a height, he gazes down from his place among the clouds; disconcerted by the unusual experience, he knows not what to do next, and can only stammer when he speaks. And that causes great entertainment, not to Thracian servant-girls or any other uneducated persons—they do not see what is going on—but to all men who have not been brought up like slaves.

These are the two types, Theodorus. There is the one who has
e been brought up in true freedom and leisure, the man you call a
philosopher; a man to whom it is no disgrace to appear simple and
good-for-nothing when he is confronted with menial tasks, when,
for instance, he doesn't know how to make a bed, or how to sweeten
a sauce or a flattering speech. Then you have the other, the man
who is keen and smart at doing all these jobs, but does not know
how to strike up a song in his turn like a free man, or how to tune
176 the strings of common speech to the fitting praise of the life of gods
and of the happy among men.

THEOD. Socrates, if your words convinced everyone as they do
me, there would be more peace and less evil on earth.

Soc. But it is not possible, Theodorus, that evil should be destroyed—for there must always be something opposed to the good;
nor is it possible that it should have its seat in heaven. But it must
inevitably haunt human life, and prowl about this earth. That is
why a man should make all haste to escape from earth to heaven;
b and escape means becoming as like God as possible; and a man
becomes like God when he becomes just and pure, with understanding. But it is not at all an easy matter, my good friend, to
persuade men that it is not for the reasons commonly alleged that
one should try to escape from wickedness and pursue virtue. It is
not in order to avoid a bad reputation and obtain a good one that
virtue should be practised and not vice; that, it seems to me, is only
c what men call 'old wives' talk'.

Let us try to put the truth in this way. In God there is no sort of
wrong whatsoever; he is supremely just, and the thing most like
him is the man who has become as just as it lies in human nature
to be. And it is here that we see whether a man is truly able, or
truly a weakling and a nonentity; for it is the realisation of this that
is genuine wisdom and goodness, while the failure to realise it is
manifest folly and wickedness. Everything else that passes for ability and wisdom has a sort of commonness—in those who wield
political power a poor cheap show, in the manual workers a matter
d of mechanical routine. If, therefore, one meets a man who practises
injustice and is blasphemous in his talk or in his life, the best thing
for him by far is that one should never grant that there is any sort
of ability about his unscrupulousness; such men are ready enough
to glory in the reproach, and think that it means not that they are
mere rubbish, cumbering the ground to no purpose, but that they
have the kind of qualities that are necessary for survival in the
community. We must therefore tell them the truth—that their very

ignorance of their true state fixes them the more firmly therein. For they do not know what is the penalty of injustice, which is the last thing of which a man should be ignorant. It is not what they suppose—scourging and death—things which they may entirely evade in spite of their wrong-doing. It is a penalty from which there is no escape.   *e*

THEOD. And what is that?

Soc. My friend, there are two patterns set up in the world. One is divine and supremely happy; the other has nothing of God in it, and is the pattern of the deepest unhappiness. This truth the evil-doer does not see; blinded by folly and utter lack of understanding, he fails to perceive that the effect of his unjust practices is to make   177 him grow more and more like the one, and less and less like the other. For this he pays the penalty of living the life that corresponds to the pattern he is coming to resemble. And if we tell him that, unless he is delivered from this 'ability' of his, when he dies the place that is pure of all evil will not receive him; that he will for ever go on living in this world a life after his own likeness[30]—a bad man tied to bad company: he will but think, 'This is the way fools talk to a clever rascal like me.'

THEOD. Oh, yes, Socrates, sure enough.

Soc. I know it, my friend. But there is one accident to which the   *b* unjust man is liable. When it comes to giving and taking an account in a private discussion of the things he disparages; when he is willing to stand his ground like a man for long enough, instead of running away like a coward, then, my friend, an odd thing happens. In the end the things he says do not satisfy even himself; that famous eloquence of his somehow dries up, and he is left looking nothing more than a child.

But we had better leave it there; all this is really a digression; and if we go on, a flood of new subjects will pour in and overwhelm   *c* our original argument. So, if you don't mind, we will go back to what we were saying before.

THEOD. As a matter of fact, Socrates, *I* like listening to this kind of talk; it is easier for a man of my years to follow. Still, if you like, let us go back to the argument.

Soc. Well, then, we were at somewhere about this point in the argument, weren't we? We were speaking of the people who assert

---

30. I.e. after death he will be condemned to further earthly lives. For the belief that the philosopher, thanks to a life spent in pursuit of knowledge and virtue, can escape this cycle of reincarnation, see *Phaedrus* 243e–257a.

a being that is in motion, and who hold that for every individual things always are whatever they seem to him to be; and we said that they were prepared to stand upon their principle in almost every case—not least in questions of what is just and right. Here they are perfectly ready to maintain that whatever any community
d   decides to be just and right, and establishes as such, actually is what is just and right for that community and for as long as it remains so established. On the other hand, when it is a question of what things are good, we no longer find anyone so heroic that he will venture to contend that whatever a community thinks useful, and establishes, really is useful, so long as it is the established order—unless, of course, he means that it is *called* 'useful'; but that would be making a game of our argument, wouldn't it?

THEOD. It would indeed.

e   Soc. Let us suppose, then, that he is not talking about the name 'useful' but has in view the thing to which it is applied.

THEOD. Agreed.

Soc. It is surely this that a government aims at when it legislates, whatever name it calls it. A community always makes such laws as are most useful to it—so far as the limits of its judgement and capacity permit.—Or do you think legislation may have some other object in view?

178   THEOD. Oh no, not at all.

Soc. And does a community always achieve this object? Or are there always a number of failures?

THEOD. It seems to me that there are failures.

Soc. Now we might put this matter in a rather different way and be still more likely to get people generally to agree with our conclusions. I mean, one might put a question about the whole class of things to which 'what is useful' belongs. These things are concerned, I take it, with future time; thus when we legislate, we make laws that are going to be useful in the time to come. This kind of thing we may properly call 'future'.

b   THEOD. Yes, certainly.

Soc. Come then, let's put a question to Protagoras (or to anyone who professes the same views): 'Now, Protagoras, "Man is the measure of all things" as you people say—of white and heavy and light and all that kind of thing without exception. He has the criterion of these things within himself; so when he thinks that they are as he experiences them, he thinks what is true and what really is for him.' Isn't that so?

THEOD. It is.

Soc. 'Then, Protagoras,' we shall say, 'what about things that are

going to be in the future? Has a man the criterion of these within   c
himself? When he thinks certain things *will be*, do they actually happen, for him, as he thought they would? Take heat, for example.
Suppose the ordinary man thinks he is going to take a fever, and that
his temperature will go up to fever point; while another man, this
time a doctor, thinks the opposite. Do we hold that the future will
confirm either the one judgement or the other? Or are we to say that
it will confirm both; that is, that for the doctor the man will not have
a temperature or be suffering from fever, while for himself he will?'

THEOD. That would be absurd.

SOC. But, when there is a question of the sweetness and dryness
of the next vintage, I presume it would always be the grower's judge-   d
ment that would carry authority, rather than that of a musician?

THEOD. Of course.

SOC. Nor again, in any question of what will be in tune or out of
tune, would the judgement of a teacher of gymnastic be superior
to that of a musician—even about what is going to seem to be in
tune to the gymnastic master himself?

THEOD. No, never.

SOC. Or suppose a dinner is being prepared. Even the guest who
is going to eat it, if he has no knowledge of cooking, will not be
able to pronounce so authoritative a verdict as the professional cook
on how nice it is going to be. I say 'going to be', because we had
better not at this stage press our point as regards what is *now*   e
pleasant to any individual, or what has been in the past. Our
question for the moment is, whether the individual himself is the
best judge, for himself, of what is going to seem and be for him in
the future. 'Or,' we will ask, 'would not you, Protagoras, predict
better than any layman about the persuasive effect that speeches
in a law-court will have upon any one of us?'

THEOD. And in fact, Socrates, this at any rate is a point on which
Protagoras used to make strong claims to superiority over other
people.

SOC. Of course he did, my dear good fellow. No one would have
paid large fees for the privilege of talking with him if he had not   179
been in the habit of persuading his pupils that he was a better judge
than any fortune-teller—or anyone else— about what was going to
be and seem to be in the future.[31]

THEOD. That's true enough.

---

31. An alternative text yields: 'if he really was in the habit of persuading his pupils
that, even about the future, neither a fortune-teller nor anyone else can judge better
than one can for oneself'.

Soc. Legislation also and 'what is useful' is concerned with the future; and it would be generally admitted to be inevitable that a city when it legislates often fails to achieve what is the most useful.

THEOD. Yes, surely.

Soc. Then we shall be giving your master fair measure if we tell
b   him that he has now got to admit that one man is wiser than another, and that it is such a man who is 'the measure'; but that I, the man with no special knowledge, have not by any means got to be a measure—a part which the recent speech in his defence was trying to force upon me, whether I liked it or not.

THEOD. Now that, Socrates, seems to me to be the chief point on which the theory is convicted of error—though it stands convicted also when it makes other men's judgements carry authority and these turn out to involve thinking that Protagoras' statements are completely untrue.

c   Soc. There is more than one point besides these, Theodorus, on which a conviction might be secured—at least so far as it is a matter of proving that not every man's judgement is true. But so long as we keep within the limits of that immediate present experience of the individual which gives rise to perceptions and to perceptual judgements, it is more difficult to convict these latter of being untrue—but perhaps I'm talking nonsense. Perhaps it is not possible to convict them at all; perhaps those who profess that they are perfectly evident and are always knowledge may be saying what really is. And it may be that our Theaetetus was not far from the
d   mark with his proposition that knowledge and perception are the same thing. We shall have to come to closer grips with the theory, as the speech on behalf of Protagoras required us to do. We shall have to consider and test this moving Being, and find whether it rings true or sounds as if it had some flaw in it. There is no small fight going on about it, anyway—and no shortage of fighting men.

THEOD. No, indeed; but in Ionia[32] it seems to be even growing, and assuming vast dimensions. On the side of this theory, the Heracleitean party is conducting a most vigorous campaign.

Soc. The more reason, then, my dear Theodorus, why we should examine it by going back to its first principle,[33] which is the way
e   they present it themselves.

THEOD. I quite agree. You know, Socrates, these Heraclitean

---

32. The central part of the west coast of Asia Minor (now Turkey). The Greek cities in this area included Ephesus, where Heraclitus was born in the sixth century B.C.

33. I.e. the principle that everything is really motion (156a).

doctrines (or, as you say, Homeric or still more ancient)—you can't discuss them in person with any of the people at Ephesus who profess to be adepts, any more than you could with a maniac. They are just like the things they say in their books—always on the move. As for abiding by what is said, or sticking to a question, or quietly answering and asking questions in turn, there is less than nothing of that in their capacity. That's an exaggeration, no doubt. I mean there isn't so much as a tiny bit of repose in these people. If you ask any one of them a question, he will pull out some little enigmatic phrase from his quiver and shoot it off at you; and if you try to make him give an account of what he has said, you will only get hit by another, full of strange turns of language. You will never reach any conclusion with any of them, ever; indeed they never reach any conclusion with each other, they are so very careful not to allow anything to be stable, either in an argument or in their own souls. I suppose they think that if they did it would be something that stands still—this being what they are totally at war with, and what they are determined to banish from the universe, if they can.

180

b

Soc. I dare say, Theodorus, you have seen these men only on the field of battle, and never been with them in times of peace—as you don't belong to their set. I expect they keep such matters to be explained at leisure to their pupils whom they want to make like themselves.

Theod. *Pupils*, my good man? There are no pupils and teachers among these people. They just spring up on their own, one here, one there, wherever they happen to catch their inspiration; and no one of them will credit another with knowing anything. As I was just going to say, you will never get these men to give an account of themselves, willingly or unwillingly. What we must do is to take their doctrine out of their hands and consider it for ourselves, as we should a problem in geometry.

c

Soc. What you say is very reasonable. This problem now, we have inherited it, have we not, from the ancients? They used poetical forms which concealed from the majority of men their real meaning, namely, that Ocean and Tethys, the origin of all things, are actually flowing streams, and nothing stands still. In more modern times, the problem is presented to us by men who, being more accomplished in these matters, plainly demonstrate their meaning so that even shoe-makers may hear and assimilate their wisdom, and give up the silly idea that some things in this world stand still while others move, learn that all things are in motion, and recognise the greatness of their instructors.

d

But I was almost forgetting, Theodorus, that there are other thinkers who have announced the opposite view; who tell us that
e 'Unmoved is the Universe',[34] and other similar statements which we hear from a Melissus[35] or a Parmenides as against the whole party of Heracleiteans. These philosophers insist that all things are One, and that this One stands still, itself within itself, having no place in which to move.

What are we to do with all these people, my friend? We have been gradually advancing till, without realising it, we have got ourselves in between the two parties; and if we don't in some way
181 manage to put up a fight and make our escape, we shall pay for it, like the people who play that game on the line in the wrestling schools, and get caught by both parties and pulled in opposite directions.

Now I think we ought to begin by examining the other party, the fluent fellows we started to pursue. If they appear to us to be talking sense, we will help them to drag us over to their side, and try to escape the others. But if those who make their stand for the whole appear to be nearer the truth, we will take refuge with them from
b the men who 'move what should not be moved'. And if it appears that neither party has a reasonable theory, then we shall be very absurd if we think that insignificant people like ourselves can have anything to say, after we have rejected the views of men who lived so long ago and possessed all wisdom. Think now, Theodorus, is it of any use for us to go forward upon such a dangerous venture?

THEOD. We can't refuse to examine the doctrines of these two schools, Socrates; that couldn't be allowed.

SOC. Then we must examine them, if *you* feel so strongly about
c it. Now it seems to me that the proper starting-point of our criticism is the nature of motion; what is this thing that they are talking about when they say that all things are in motion? I mean, for example, are they referring to one form of motion only, or, as I think, to two—but don't let this be only what *I* think. You commit yourself as well, so that we may come to grief together, if need be. Tell me, do you call it 'motion' when a thing changes from one place to another or turns round in the same place?

THEOD. I do, yes.

SOC. Here then is one form of motion. Then supposing a thing
d remains in the same place, but grows old, or becomes black instead

---

34. Both the text and the sense of this quotation are uncertain.
35. Melissus of Samos was a fifth-century follower of Parmenides.

of white, or hard instead of soft, or undergoes any other alteration; isn't it right to say that here we have motion in another form?

THEOD. Unquestionably.

SOC. Then I now have two forms of motion, alteration and spatial movement.[36]

THEOD. Yes; and that's quite correct.

SOC. Then now that we have made this distinction, let us have a talk with the people who allege that all things are in motion. Let us ask them, 'Do you hold that everything is in motion in both ways, that is, that it both moves through space and undergoes alteration? Or do you suggest that some things are in motion in both ways, and some only in one or the other?'

THEOD. Heaven knows, I can't answer that. I suppose they would say, in both ways.

SOC. Yes; otherwise, my friend, it will turn out that, in their view, things are both moving and standing still; and it will be no more correct to say that all things are in motion than to say that all things stand still.

THEOD. That's perfectly true.

SOC. Then since they must be in motion, and there is no such thing anywhere as absence of motion, it follows that all things are always in every kind of motion.

THEOD. Yes, that must be so.

SOC. Then I want you to consider this point in their theory. As we were saying, they hold that the genesis of things such as warmth and whiteness occurs when each of them is moving, together with a perception, in the space between the active and passive factors: the passive factor thereby becoming percipient, but not a perception, while the active factor becomes such or such, but not a quality—isn't that so? But perhaps 'quality' seems a strange word to you; perhaps you don't quite understand it as a general expression.[37] So I will talk about particular cases. What I mean is that the

36. In the above passage the words *kinēsis, kineisthai*, translated 'motion', 'be in motion', take on a wider sense than they would normally have. Normally they would signify some kind of movement, especially spatial movement, but the Heraclitean philosophy makes the flowing movement of a river the symbol of change in general and change in general is what 'motion' becomes when alteration is subsumed under it. For alteration too is taken widely, to include growing old as well as change of quality or character. The translations 'motion' and 'alteration' reproduce quite well the sense of language being stretched.

37. Socrates apologizes for the strangeness of the expression because this is the first occurrence in Greek of the word *poiotēs*, 'quality' or 'what-sort-ness', coined by Plato from the interrogative adjective *poios*, 'of what sort?'. Cicero, *Academica* I 24–6, was

b active factor becomes not warmth or whiteness, but warm and
white; and so on. You will remember, perhaps, that we said in the
earlier stages of the argument that there is nothing which in itself
is just one thing; and that this applies also to the active and passive
factors. It is by the association of the two with one another that they
generate perceptions and the things perceived; and in so doing,
the active factor becomes such and such, while the passive factor
becomes percipient.

THEOD. Yes, I remember that, of course.

c   SOC. Then we need not concern ourselves about other points in
their doctrine, whether they mean what we say or something else.
We must keep our eyes simply upon the object of our discussion.
We must ask them this question: 'According to you, all things move
and flow; isn't that so?'

THEOD. Yes.

SOC. And they have both the motions that we distinguished,
that is to say, they both move and alter?

THEOD. That must be so, if they are to be wholly and completely
in motion.

SOC. Now if they were only moving through space and not alter-
ing, we should presumably be able to say *what* the moving things
flow?[38] Or how do we express it?

THEOD. That's all right.

d   SOC. But since not even this abides, that what flows flows white;
but rather it is in process of change, so that there is flux of this very
thing also, the whiteness, and it is passing over into another colour,
lest it be convicted of standing still in this respect—since that is so,
is it possible to give any name to a colour which will properly apply
to it?

THEOD. I don't see how one could, Socrates; nor yet surely to
anything else of that kind, if, being in flux, it is always quietly
slipping away as you speak?

SOC. And what about any particular kind of perception; for exam-
e   ple, seeing or hearing? Does it ever abide, and remain seeing or
hearing?

THEOD. It ought not to, certainly, if all things are in motion.

---

imitating this passage when he coined *qualitas* from *qualis*, the Latin equivalent of
poios. Ultimately, therefore, the *Theaetetus* is responsible for our word 'quality'.

38. I.e. 'what they *are*', as we should say. A specially conscientious attempt to speak
the language proper to the theory of flux. The words which follow apologise for the
oddness of the result.

Soc. Then we may not call anything seeing rather than not-seeing; nor indeed may we call it any other perception rather than not—if it be admitted that all things are in motion in every way?

Theod. No, we may not.

Soc. Yet Theaetetus and I said that knowledge was perception?

Theod. You did.

Soc. And so our answer to the question, 'What is knowledge?' gave something which is no more knowledge than not.

Theod. It seems as if it did.   *183*

Soc. A fine way this turns out to be of making our answer right. We were most anxious to prove that all things are in motion, in order to make that answer come out correct; but what has really emerged is that, if all things are in motion, every answer, on whatever subject, is equally correct, both 'it is thus' and 'it is not thus'— or if you like 'becomes', as we don't want to use any expressions which will bring our friends to a stand-still.

Theod. You are quite right.

Soc. Well, yes, Theodorus, except that I said 'thus' and 'not thus'. One must not use even the word 'thus'; for this 'thus' would no longer be in motion; nor yet 'not thus' for here again there is no motion. The exponents of this theory need to establish some other language; as it is, they have no words that are consistent with their hypothesis—unless it would perhaps suit them best to use 'not at all thus' in a quite indefinite sense.[39]   *b*

Theod. That would at least be an idiom most appropriate to them.

Soc. Then we are set free from your friend, Theodorus. We do not yet concede to him that every man is the measure of all things, if he be not a man of understanding. And we are not going to grant that knowledge is perception, not at any rate on the line of inquiry which supposes that all things are in motion; we are not going to grant it unless Theaetetus here has some other way of stating it.   *c*

Theod. That's very good hearing, Socrates, for when these matters were concluded I was to be set free from my task of answering you, according to our agreement, which specified the end of the discussion of Protagoras' theory.

---

39. I.e. presumably, a pure contradictory: it denies one 'thus' without implying any other 'thus'. There is some textual uncertainty about the form of phrasing left open to the Heracliteans, but what is required to block any implication from e.g. 'not white' to 'not white but another colour' is something that simply denies the presence of white.

THEAET. Oh, no, indeed, Theodorus! Not till you and Socrates
d   have done what you proposed just now, and dealt with the other
side, the people who say that the Universe stands still.

THEOD. What's this, Theaetetus? You at your age teaching your
elders to be unjust and break their agreements? What you have got
to do is to prepare to render account to Socrates yourself for the
rest of the discussion.

THEAET. All right, if he likes. But I would rather have listened to
a discussion of these views.

THEOD. Well, challenging Socrates to an argument is like inviting
'cavalry into the plain'. So ask your questions and you shall hear.

Soc. But I don't think, Theodorus, that I am going to be per-
e   suaded by Theaetetus to do what he demands.

THEOD. But what is it makes you unwilling?

Soc. Shame. I am afraid our criticism might be a very cheap
affair. And if I feel like this before the many who have made the
universe one and unmoved, Melissus and the rest of them, I feel it
still more in the face of the One—Parmenides. Parmenides seems
to me, in the words of Homer, to be 'reverend' and 'awful'. I met
him when I was very young and he was a very old man; and he
184   seemed to me to have a wholly noble depth.[40] So I am afraid we
might not understand even what he says; still less should we attain
to his real thought. Above all, I am afraid that the very object of
our discussion, the nature of knowledge, might be left unexamined
amid the crowd of theories that will rush in upon us if we admit
them; especially as the theory we have now brought up is one
which involves unmanageably vast issues. To treat it as a side-
show, would be insult and injury; while if it is adequately discussed,
it is likely to spread out until it completely eclipses the problem of
knowledge. We must not do either. What we must do is to make
b   use of our midwife's art to deliver Theaetetus of the thoughts which
he has conceived about the nature of knowledge.

THEOD. Well, if that is what you think proper, it must be done.

Soc. Now, Theaetetus, I want you to think about one point in
what has been said. Your answer was that knowledge is perception,
wasn't it?

---

40. The reference is probably not to an actual historical meeting but to the discussion
between Socrates and Parmenides in Plato's *Parmenides*. 'Depth' in Greek usage
alludes not only to profundity of thought but also to the unruffled composure
which is the proper bearing of a philosopher. In contrast to the unsteadiness of
the Heracliteans (179e–180c), Parmenides' mind is one to which it is difficult for
understanding or critical questioning to penetrate.

THEAET. Yes.

Soc. Now supposing you were asked: 'With what does a man see white and black, and with what does he hear high and low notes?' You would reply, I imagine, 'With his eyes and ears.'

THEAET. I should, yes.

Soc. Now as a rule it is no sign of ill-breeding to be easy in the *c* use of language and take no particular care in one's choice of words; it is rather the opposite that gives a man away. But such exactness is sometimes necessary; and it is necessary here, for example, to fasten upon something in your answer that is not correct. Think now. Is it more correct to say that the eyes are that *with* which we see, or that *through* which we see? Do we hear *with* the ears or *through* the ears?

THEAET. Well, I should think, Socrates, that it is '*through* which' we perceive in each case, rather than '*with* which.'

Soc. Yes, my son. It would be a very strange thing, I must say, *d* if there were a number of senses sitting inside us as if we were Wooden Horses, and there were not some single form, soul or whatever one ought to call it, to which all these converge—something *with* which, *through* the senses, as if they were instruments, we perceive all that is perceptible.

THEAET. That sounds to me better than the other way of putting it.

Soc. Now the reason why I am being so precise with you is this. I want to know if it is with one and the same part of ourselves that we reach, through our eyes to white and black, and through the other means to yet further things; and whether, if asked, you will *e* be able to refer all these to the body. But perhaps it would be better if you stated the answers yourself, rather than that I should busy myself on your behalf. Tell me: the instruments through which you perceive hot, hard, light, sweet—do you consider that they all belong to the body? Or can they be referred elsewhere?

THEAET. No, they all belong to the body.

Soc. And are you also willing to admit that what you perceive through one power, you can't perceive through another? For in- *185* stance, what you perceive through hearing, you couldn't perceive through sight, and similarly what you perceive through sight you couldn't perceive through hearing?

THEAET. I could hardly refuse to grant that.

Soc. Then suppose you think something about both; you can't possibly be having a perception about both, either through one of these instruments or through the other?

THEAET. No.

Soc. Now take a sound and a colour. First of all, don't you think this same thing about both of them, namely, that they both are?

THEAET. I do.

Soc. Also that each of them is different from the other and the same as itself?

b　THEAET. Of course.

Soc. And that both together are two, and each of them is one?

THEAET. Yes, I think that too.

Soc. Are you also able to consider whether they are like or unlike each other?

THEAET. Yes, I may be.

Soc. Now what is it through which you think all these things about them? It is not possible, you see, to grasp what is common to both either through sight or through hearing. Let us consider another thing which will show the truth of what we are saying. Suppose it were possible to enquire whether both are salty or not.

c　You can tell me, of course, with what you would examine them. It would clearly be neither sight nor hearing, but something else.

THEAET. Yes, of course; the power which functions through the tongue.

Soc. Good. Now through what does that power function which reveals to you what is common in the case both of all things and of these two—I mean that which you express by the words 'is' and 'is not' and the other terms used in our questions about them just now? What kind of instruments will you assign for all these? Through what does that which is percipient in us perceive all of them?

THEAET. You mean being and not-being, likeness and unlike-

d　ness, same and different; also one, and any other number applied to them. And obviously too your question is about odd and even, and all that is involved with these attributes; and you want to know through what bodily instruments we perceive all these with the soul.

Soc. You follow me exceedingly well, Theaetetus. These are just the things I am asking about.

THEAET. But *I* couldn't possibly say. All I can tell you is that it doesn't seem to me that for these things there is any special instrument at all, as there is for the others. It seems to me that in inves-

e　tigating the common features of everything the soul functions through itself.

Soc. Yes, Theaetetus, you would say that, because you are hand-

some and not ugly as Theodorus would have it.[41] For handsome is
as handsome says. And besides being handsome, you have done
me a good turn; you have saved me a vast amount of talk if it seems
to you that, while the soul considers some things through the bodily
powers, there are others which it considers alone and through itself.
This was what I thought myself, but I wanted you to think it too.

THEAET. Well, it does seem to me to be so.   *186*

Soc. Now in which class do you put being? For that, above all,
is something that accompanies everything.

THEAET. I should put it among the things which the soul itself
reaches out after by itself.

Soc. Also like and unlike, same and different?

THEAET. Yes.

Soc. What about beautiful and ugly, good and bad?

THEAET. Yes, these too; in these, above all, I think the soul examines the being they have as compared with one another. Here it
seems to be making a calculation within itself of past and present   *b*
in relation to future.

Soc. Not so fast, now. Wouldn't you say that it is through touch
that the soul perceives the hardness of what is hard, and similarly
the softness of what is soft?

THEAET. Yes.

Soc. But as regards their being—the fact that they are—their
opposition to one another, and the being, again, of this opposition,
the matter is different. Here the soul itself attempts to reach a
decision for us by rising to compare them with one another.

THEAET. Yes, undoubtedly.

Soc. And thus there are some things which all creatures, men
and animals alike, are naturally able to perceive as soon as they are   *c*
born; I mean, the experiences which reach the soul through the
body. But calculations regarding their being and their advanta-
geousness come, when they do, only as the result of a long and
arduous development, involving a good deal of trouble and education.

THEAET. Yes, that certainly is so.

Soc. Now is it possible for someone who does not even get at
being to get at truth?

THEAET. No; it's impossible.

Soc. And if a man fails to get at the truth of a thing, will he ever
be a person who knows that thing?

41. Cf. 143e.

d   THEAET. I don't see how, Socrates.

Soc. Then knowledge is to be found not in the experiences but in the process of reasoning about them; it is here, seemingly, not in the experiences, that it is possible to grasp being and truth.

THEAET. So it appears.

Soc. Then in the face of such differences, would you call both by the same name?

THEAET. One would certainly have no right to.

Soc. Now what name do you give to the former—seeing, hearing, smelling, feeling cold or warm?

e   THEAET. I call that perceiving—what else could I call it?

Soc. So the whole lot taken together you call perception?

THEAET. Necessarily.

Soc. Which, we say, has no share in the grasping of truth, since it has none in the grasping of being.

THEAET. No, it has none.

Soc. So it has no share in knowledge either.

THEAET. No.

Soc. Then, Theaetetus, perception and knowledge could never be the same thing.

THEAET. No, apparently not, Socrates; we have now got the clearest possible proof that knowledge is something different from perception.

187   Soc. But our object in beginning this discussion was not to find out what knowledge is not, but to find out what it is. However, we have made a little progress. We shall not now look for knowledge in sense-perception at all, but in whatever we call that activity of the soul when it is busy by itself about the things which are.

THEAET. Well, the name, Socrates, I suppose is judgement.

Soc. Your opinion, my dear lad, is correct. Now look back to the
b   beginning. Wipe out all that we have said hitherto, and see if you can see any better from where you have now progressed to. Tell me again, what is knowledge?

THEAET. Well, Socrates, one can't say that it is judgement in general, because there is also false judgement— but true judgement may well be knowledge. So let that be my answer. If the same thing happens again, and we find, as we go on, that it turns out not to be so, we'll try something else.

Soc. And even so, Theaetetus, you have answered me in the way one ought—with a good will, and not reluctantly, as you did
c   at first. If we continue like this, one of two things will happen.

Either we shall find what we are going out after; or we shall be less inclined to think we know things which we don't know at all—and even that would be a reward we could not fairly be dissatisfied with. Now what is this that you say? There are two forms of judgement, true and false; and your definition is that true judgement is knowledge?

THEAET. Yes. That is how it looks to me now.

Soc. Now I wonder if it's worth while, at this stage, to go back to an old point about judgement—

THEAET. What point do you mean?

Soc. I have something on my mind which has often bothered   *d*
me before, and got me into great difficulty, both in my own thought and in discussion with other people—I mean, I can't say what it is, this experience we have, and how it arises in us.

THEAET. What experience?

Soc. Judging what is false. Even now, you know, I'm still considering; I'm in two minds whether to let it go or whether to look into it in a different manner from a short while ago.

THEAET. Why not, Socrates, if this appears for any reason to be the right thing to do? As you and Theodorus were saying just now, and quite rightly, when you were talking about leisure, we are not pressed for time in talk of this kind.

Soc. A very proper reminder. Perhaps it would not be a bad   *e*
moment to go back upon our tracks. It is better to accomplish a little well than a great deal unsatisfactorily.

THEAET. Yes, it certainly is.

Soc. Now how are we to proceed? And actually what is it that we are saying? We claim, don't we, that false judgement repeatedly occurs and one of us judges falsely, the other truly, as if it was in the nature of things for this to happen?

THEAET. That is what we claim.

Soc. Now isn't it true about all things, together or individually,   *188*
that we must either know them or not know them? I am ignoring for the moment the intermediate conditions of learning and forgetting, as they don't affect the argument here.

THEAET. Of course, Socrates, in that case there is no alternative. With each thing we either know it or we do not.

Soc. Then when a man judges, the objects of his judgement are necessarily either things which he knows or things which he doesn't know?

THEAET. Yes, that must be so.

Soc. Yet if he knows a thing, it is impossible that he should not
b know it; or if he does not know it, he cannot know it.

THEAET. Yes, of course.

Soc. Now take the man who judges what is false. Is he thinking
that things which he knows are not these things but some other
things which he knows—so that knowing both he is ignorant of
both?

THEAET. But that would be impossible, Socrates.

Soc. Then is he imagining that things which he doesn't know
are other things which he doesn't know? Is it possible that a man
who knows neither Theaetetus nor Socrates should take it into his
head that Socrates is Theaetetus or Theaetetus Socrates?

c THEAET. I don't see how that could happen.

Soc. But a man certainly doesn't think that things he knows are
things he does not know, or again that things he doesn't know are
things he knows.

THEAET. No, that would be a very odd thing.

Soc. Then in what way is false judgement still possible? There
is evidently no possibility of judgement outside the cases we have
mentioned, since everything is either what we know or what we
don't know; and within these limits there appears to be no place
for false judgement to be possible.

THEAET. That's perfectly true.

Soc. Then perhaps we had better take up a different line of
enquiry; perhaps we should proceed not by way of knowing and
d not-knowing, but by way of being and not-being?

THEAET. How do you mean?

Soc. Perhaps the simple fact is this: it is when a man judges
about anything things which are not, that he is inevitably judging
falsely, no matter what may be the nature of his thought in other
respects.

THEAET. That again is very plausible, Socrates.

Soc. Now how will that be? What are we going to say, Theaetetus, if somebody sets about examining us, and we are asked, 'Is
what these words express possible for anyone? Can a man judge
what is not, either about one of the things which are, or just by
e itself?' I suppose we shall reply, 'Yes, when he is thinking, but
thinking what is not true.' Or how shall we answer?

THEAET. That's our answer.

Soc. Now does this kind of thing happen elsewhere?

THEAET. What kind of thing?

Soc. Well, for instance, that a man sees something, yet sees nothing.

Theaet. How could he?

Soc. On the contrary, in fact, if he is seeing any one thing, he must be seeing a thing which is. Or do you think that a 'one' can be found among the things which are not?

Theaet. I certainly don't.

Soc. Then a man who is seeing any one thing is seeing something which is?

Theaet. Apparently.

Soc. It also follows that a man who is hearing anything is hearing   189
some one thing and something which is.

Theaet. Yes.

Soc. And a man who is touching anything is touching some one thing, and a thing which is, if it is one?

Theaet. Yes, that also follows.

Soc. And a man who is judging is judging some one thing, is he not?

Theaet. Necessarily.

Soc. And a man who is judging some one thing is judging something which is?

Theaet. I grant that.

Soc. Then that means that a man who is judging something which is not is judging nothing?

Theaet. So it appears.

Soc. But a man who is judging nothing is not judging at all.

Theaet. That seems clear.

Soc. And so it is not possible to judge what is not, either about   b
the things which are or just by itself.

Theaet. Apparently not.

Soc. False judgement, then, is something different from judging things which are not?

Theaet. It looks as if it were.

Soc. Then neither on this approach nor on the one we followed just now does false judgement exist in us.

Theaet. No, indeed.

Soc. Then is it in this way that the thing we call by that name arises?

Theaet. How?

Soc. We say that there is false judgement, a kind of 'other-judging', when a man, in place of one of the things that are, has   c substituted in his thought another of the things that are and asserts that it is.[42] In this way, he is always judging something which is, but judges one thing in place of another; and having missed the thing which was the object of his consideration, he might fairly be called one who judges falsely.

THEAET. Now you seem to me to have got it quite right. When a man judges 'ugly' instead of 'beautiful', or 'beautiful' instead of 'ugly', then he is truly judging what is false.

Soc. Evidently, Theaetetus, you have not much opinion of me; you don't find me at all alarming.

THEAET. What in particular makes you say that?

Soc. Well, I suppose you don't think me capable of taking up your 'truly false', and asking you whether it is possible that a thing should be slowly swift, or heavily light, or whether anything else can possibly occur in a way not in accordance with its own nature but in accordance with that of its opposite and contrary to itself. But let that pass; I don't want your boldness to go unrewarded. You like the suggestion, you say, that false judgement is 'other-judging'?

THEAET. Yes, I do.

Soc. Then, according to your judgement, it is possible to set down a thing in one's thought as another thing and not itself?

THEAET. Surely it is.

Soc. Now when a man's thought is accomplishing this, isn't it

---

42. In the manuscripts on which we rely for the *Theaetetus*, this sentence does not make grammatical sense; we have to supply by conjecture a word or phrase which an earlier copyist inadvertently left out. With the standard supplement (*ti*) the sentence is standardly translated 'when a man asserts that one of the things which are is another of the things which are, having substituted one for the other in his thought'. The objection to this conjecture is that it builds into the initial description of 'other-judging' the very feature which, when exposed in the sequel, will be its downfall. For the criticism which follows is designed to show that one cannot judge F to be the case in place of G without judging, absurdly, that F is G. Moreover, the standard translation does not fit Socrates' next sentence or the examples in Theaetetus' reply. The version given above fits both, but it supposes a nonstandard supplement of my own (*anti tinos*). Some scholars think it possible to accept the standard conjecture and give it a nonstandard translation, tantamount to mine and so fitting the requirements of the context. If this third option is viable, it might be appropriate to conclude that Plato designed the sentence to be ambiguous between the nonstandard and the standard understanding of it, so that, when you read the whole passage 189b–190e in the original Greek, the criticism of the definition of false judgement as 'other-judging' makes you experience the process of substituting one meaning for the other in your thought.

essential that he should be thinking of either one or both of these two things?

THEAET. It is essential; either both together, or each in turn.

Soc. Very good. Now by 'thinking' do you mean the same as I do?

THEAET. What do you mean by it?

Soc. A talk which the soul has with itself about the objects under its consideration. Of course, I'm only telling you my idea in all ignorance; but this is the kind of picture I have of it. It seems to me that the soul when it thinks is simply carrying on a discussion in which it asks itself questions and answers them itself, affirms and denies. And when it arrives at something definite, either by a gradual process or a sudden leap, when it affirms one thing consistently and without divided counsel, we call this its judgement. So, in my view, to judge is to make a statement, and a judgement is a statement which is not addressed to another person or spoken aloud, but silently addressed to oneself. And what do you think?

190

THEAET. I agree with that.

Soc. So that when a man judges one thing to be another, what he is doing, apparently, is to say to himself that the one thing is the other.

THEAET. Yes, of course.

b

Soc. Now try to think if you have ever said to yourself 'Surely the beautiful is ugly',[43] or 'The unjust is certainly just'. Or—to put it in the most general terms—have you ever tried to persuade yourself that 'Surely one thing is another'? Wouldn't the very opposite of this be the truth? Wouldn't the truth be that not even in your sleep have you ever gone so far as to say to yourself 'No doubt the odd is even', or anything of that kind?

THEAET. Yes, that's so.

---

43. 'The beautiful is ugly' may mean that some particular beautiful thing is ugly, but it can also, in Greek idiom, be a way of saying that beauty is ugliness. Correspondingly with examples like 'A cow is a horse' below: this may mean that some particular cow is a horse, but it can also, as in English idiom, be a general statement equivalent to 'Cows are horses'. In favour of the second construal in each case is the fact that 'beautiful' and 'ugly' came into the discussion at 189c as the predicate term in a mistaken judgement. Moreover, the first construal fails to illustrate Socrates' contention that the man says of two distinct things that the one is the other. Accordingly, it is the second construal which is followed in the Introduction, p. 83 ff. 'Beauty is ugliness' could also be put into English as 'A beautiful thing is an ugly thing' provided that is read in the same way as 'A cow is a horse', i.e. as equivalent to the general statement 'Beautiful things are ugly'.

c   Soc. And do you think that anyone else, in his right mind or out of it, ever ventured seriously to tell himself, with the hope of winning his own assent, that 'A cow must be a horse' or 'Two must be one'?

THEAET. No, indeed I don't.

Soc. Well, then, if to make a statement to oneself is to judge, no one who makes a statement, that is, a judgement, about both things, getting hold of both with his soul, can state, or judge, that one is the other. And you, in your turn, must pass this form of words.[44] What I mean by it is this: no one judges 'The ugly is

d   beautiful' or makes any other such judgement.

THEAET. All right, Socrates, I pass it; and I think you're right.

Soc. Thus a man who has both things before his mind when he judges cannot possibly judge that one is the other.

THEAET. So it seems.

Soc. But if he has only one of them before his mind in judging, and the other is not present to him at all, he will never judge that one is the other.

THEAET. That's true. For he would have to have hold also of the one that is not present to his judgement.

Soc. Then 'other-judging' is not possible for anyone either when

e   he has both things present to him in judgement or when he has one only. So, if anyone is going to define false judgement as 'hetero-doxy',[45] he will be saying nothing. The existence of false judgement in us cannot be shown in this way any more than by our previous approaches.

THEAET. It seems not.

Soc. And yet, Theaetetus, if it is not shown to exist, we shall be driven into admitting a number of absurdities.

THEAET. And what would they be?

Soc. I am not going to tell you until I have tried every possible way of looking at this matter. I should be ashamed to see us forced

191   into making the kind of admissions I mean while we are still in difficulties. If we find what we're after, and become free men, then we will turn round and talk about how these things happen to other

---

44. In Greek the opposition between 'the one' and 'the other' is expressed by the repetition of the word meaning 'other', so that the phrase can also be understood as the unparadoxical tautology 'the other is other'. As Socrates refrained at 189cd from taking up the paradoxical construal of Theaetetus' 'truly false', so Theaetetus must refrain from taking up the unparadoxical construal of Socrates' 'one is the other'.

45. A transliteration of a variant Greek expression for 'other-judging'.

people—having secured our own persons against ridicule. While if we can't find any way of extricating ourselves, then I suppose we shall be laid low, like sea-sick passengers, and give ourselves into the hands of the argument and let it trample all over us and do what it likes with us. And now let me tell you where I see a way still open to this enquiry.

THEAET. Yes, do tell me.

SOC. I am going to maintain that we were wrong to agree that it is impossible for a man to be in error through judging that things he knows are things he doesn't know. In a way, it is possible.   *b*

THEAET. Now I wonder if you mean the same thing as I too suspected at the time when we suggested it was like that—I mean, that sometimes I, who know Socrates, have seen someone else in the distance whom I don't know and thought it to be Socrates whom I do know. In a case like that, the sort of thing you are referring to does happen.

SOC. But didn't we recoil from this suggestion because it made us not know, when we do know, things which we know?

THEAET. Yes, we certainly did.

SOC. Then don't let us put the case in that way; let's try another way. It may prove amenable or it may be obstinate; but the fact is   *c* we are in such an extremity that we need to turn every argument over and over and test it from all sides. Now see if there is anything in this. Is it possible to learn something you didn't know before?

THEAET. Surely it is.

SOC. And again another and yet another thing?

THEAET. Well, why not?

SOC. Now I want you to suppose, for the sake of the argument, that we have in our souls a block of wax, larger in one person, smaller in another, and of purer wax in one case, dirtier in another; in some men rather hard, in others rather soft, while in some it is   *d* of the proper consistency.

THEAET. All right, I'm supposing that.

SOC. We may look upon it, then, as a gift of Memory, the mother of the Muses. We make impressions upon this of everything we wish to remember among the things we have seen or heard or thought of ourselves; we hold the wax under our perceptions and thoughts and take a stamp from them, in the way in which we take the imprints of signet rings. Whatever is impressed upon the wax we remember and know so long as the image remains in the wax; whatever is obliterated or cannot be impressed, we forget and do   *e* not know.

THEAET. Let that be our supposition.

Soc. Then take the case of a man who knows these things, but is also considering something he is seeing or hearing; and see if he might judge falsely in this way.

THEAET. In what kind of way?

Soc. In thinking, of things which he knows, sometimes that they are things which he knows and sometimes that they are things which he doesn't know—these cases being what at an earlier stage we wrongly admitted to be impossible.

THEAET. And what do you say now?

192   Soc. We must begin this discussion by making certain distinctions. We must make it clear that it is impossible to think (1) that a thing you know, because you possess the record of it in your soul, but which you are not perceiving, is another thing which you know—you have its imprint too—but are not perceiving, (2) that a thing you know is something you do not know and do not have the seal of, (3) that a thing you don't know is another thing you don't know, (4) that a thing you don't know is a thing you know.

Again, it is impossible to think (1) that a thing you are perceiving is another thing that you are perceiving, (2) that a thing you are perceiving is a thing which you are not perceiving, (3) that a thing
b   you are not perceiving is another thing you are not perceiving, (4) that a thing you are not perceiving is a thing you are perceiving.

Yet again, it is impossible to think (1) that a thing you both know and are perceiving, when you are holding its signature in line with your perception of it, is another thing which you know and are perceiving, and whose signature you keep in line with the perception (this indeed is even more impossible than the former cases, if that can be), (2) that a thing which you both know and are perceiving, and the record of which you are keeping in its true line, is another thing you know, (3) that a thing you both know and are perceiving and of which you have the record correctly in line as before, is another thing you are perceiving, (4) that a thing you
c   neither know nor are perceiving is another thing you neither know nor perceive, (5) that a thing you neither know nor perceive is another thing you don't know, (6) that a thing you neither know nor perceive is another thing you are not perceiving.

In all these cases, it is a sheer impossibility that there should be false judgement. It remains that it arises, if anywhere, in the cases I am just going to tell you.

THEAET. What are they? Perhaps I may understand a little better from them; at present, I don't follow.

Soc. In these cases of things you know: when you think (1) that they are other things you know and are perceiving, (2) that they are things you don't know but are perceiving, (3) that things you both know and are perceiving are other things you both know and are perceiving.

d

Theaet. Well, now you have left me further behind than ever.

Soc. I'll go over it again in another way. I know Theodorus and remember within myself what he is like; and in the same way I know Theaetetus. But sometimes I am seeing them and sometimes not; sometimes I am touching them, and sometimes not; or I may hear them or perceive them through some other sense, while at other times I have no perception about you two at all, but remember you none the less, and know you within myself—isn't that so?

Theaet. Yes, certainly.

e

Soc. Now please take this first point that I want to make clear to you—that we sometimes perceive and sometimes do not perceive the things that we know.

Theaet. That's true.

Soc. Then as regards the things we don't know, we often don't perceive them either, but often we only perceive them.

Theaet. That is so, also.

Soc. Now see if you can follow me a little better. Supposing Socrates knows both Theodorus and Theaetetus, but is not seeing either of them, or having any other perception about them: he could never in that case judge within himself that Theaetetus was Theodorus. Is that sense or not?

193

Theaet. Yes, that's quite true.

Soc. This, then, was the first of the cases I was speaking of.

Theaet. It was.

Soc. Secondly then. Supposing I am acquainted with one of you and not with the other, and am perceiving neither of you: in that case, I could never think the one I do know to be the one I don't know.

Theaet. That is so.

Soc. Thirdly, supposing I am not acquainted with either of you, and am not perceiving either of you: I could not possibly think that one of you, whom I don't know, is another of you whom I don't know. Now will you please take it that you have heard all over again in succession the other cases described before—the cases in which I shall never judge falsely about you and Theodorus, either when I am familiar or when I am unfamiliar with both of you; or when I know one and not the other. And similarly with perceptions, if you follow me.

b

THEAET. I follow.

Soc. So there remains the possibility of false judgement in this case. I know both you and Theodorus; I have your signs upon that
c   block of wax, like the imprints of rings. Then I see you both in the distance, but cannot see you well enough; but I am in a hurry to refer the proper sign to the proper visual perception, and so get this fitted into the trace of itself, that recognition may take place. This I fail to do; I get them out of line, applying the visual perception of the one to the sign of the other. It is like people putting their shoes on the wrong feet, or like what happens when we look at
d   things in mirrors, when left and right change places. It is then that 'heterodoxy' or false judgement arises.

THEAET. Yes, that seems very likely, Socrates; it is an awfully good description of what happens to the judgement.

Soc. Then, again, supposing I know both of you, and am also perceiving one of you, and not the other, but am not keeping my knowledge of the former in line with my perception—that's the expression I used before and you didn't understand me then.

THEAET. No, I certainly didn't.

Soc. Well, I was saying that if you know one man and perceive
e   him as well, and keep your knowledge of him in line with your perception, you will never take him for some other person whom you know and are perceiving, and the knowledge of whom you are holding straight with the perception. Wasn't that so?

THEAET. Yes.

Soc. There remained, I take it, the case we have just mentioned where false judgement arises in the following manner: you know
194   both men and you are looking at both, or having some other perception of them; and you don't hold the two signs each in line with its own perception, but like a bad archer you shoot beside the mark and miss—which is precisely what we call falsehood.

THEAET. Naturally so.

Soc. And when for one of the signs there is also a present perception but there is not for the other, and you try to fit to the present perception the sign belonging to the absent perception, in all such cases thought is in error.

We may sum up thus: it seems that in the case of things we do
b   not know and have never perceived, there is no possibility of error or of false judgement, if what we are saying is at all sound; it is in cases where we both know things and are perceiving them that judgement is erratic and varies between truth and falsity. When it brings together the proper stamps and imprints directly and in

straight lines, it is true; when it does so obliquely and crosswise, it is false.

THEAET. Well, isn't that beautiful, Socrates?

Soc. Ah, when you've heard what is coming next, you will say *c*
so all the more. For true judgement is beautiful, right enough, and error is ugly.

THEAET. No doubt about that.

Soc. Well, this, then, they say, is why the two things occur. In some men, the wax in the soul is deep and abundant, smooth and worked to the proper consistency; and when the things that come through the senses are imprinted upon this 'heart' of the soul—as Homer calls it, hinting at the likeness to the wax[46]—the signs that are made in it are lasting, because they are clear and have sufficient *d*
depth. Men with such souls learn easily and remember what they learn; they do not get the signs out of line with the perceptions, but judge truly. As the signs are distinct and there is plenty of room for them, they quickly assign each thing to its own impress in the wax—the things in question being, of course, what we call the things that are and these people being the ones we call wise.

Or do you feel any doubts about this?

THEAET. No, I find it extraordinarily convincing.

Soc. But it is a different matter when a man's 'heart' is 'shaggy' *e*
(the kind of heart our marvellously knowing poet praises), or when it is dirty and of impure wax; or when it is very soft or hard. Persons in whom the wax is soft are quick to learn but quick to forget; when the wax is hard, the opposite happens. Those in whom it is 'shaggy' and rugged, a stony thing with earth or filth mixed all through it, have indistinct impressions. So too if the wax is hard, for then the impressions have no depth; similarly they are indistinct if the wax is soft, because they quickly run together and are blurred. If, in 195
addition to all this, the impresses in the wax are crowded upon each other for lack of space, because it is only some little scrap of a soul, they are even more indistinct. All such people are liable to false judgement. When they see or hear or think of anything, they can't quickly allot each thing to each impress; they are slow and allot things to impresses which do not belong to them, misseeing, mishearing and misthinking most of them—and these in turn are the ones we describe as in error about the things that are and ignorant.

---

46. The word for 'heart' attributed to Homer here is *kear*, which has a superficial resemblance to the word for wax, *kēros*.

b   THEAET. That's exactly it, Socrates; no man could improve on your account.

SOC. Then are we to say that false judgements do exist in us?

THEAET. Yes, most emphatically.

SOC. And true ones, of course?

THEAET. And true ones.

SOC. And we think we have now reached a satisfactory agreement, when we say that these two kinds of judgement certainly exist?

THEAET. There's no earthly doubt about it, Socrates.

SOC. Theaetetus, I'm afraid a garrulous man is really an awful nuisance.

THEAET. Why, what are you talking about?

c   SOC. I'm annoyed at my own stupidity—my own true garrulousness.[47] What else could you call it when a man will keep dragging arguments up and down, because he is too slow-witted to reach any conviction, and will not be pulled off any of them?

THEAET. But why should *you* be annoyed?

SOC. I am not only annoyed; I am alarmed. I am afraid of what I may say if someone asks me: 'So, Socrates, you've discovered false judgement, have you? You have found that it arises not in the relation of perceptions to one another, or of thoughts to one an-

d   other, but in the connecting of perception with thought?' I believe I am very likely to say 'Yes', with an air of flattering myself upon our having made some beautiful discovery.

THEAET. Well, Socrates, what you have just shown us looks to me quite a presentable thing anyway.

SOC. 'You mean,' he goes on, 'that we would never suppose that a man we are merely thinking of but not seeing is a horse which again we are not seeing or touching, but just thinking of and not perceiving anything else about it?' I suppose I shall agree that we do mean this.

THEAET. Yes, and quite rightly.

e   SOC. 'Well then,' he goes on, 'doesn't it follow from this theory that a man couldn't possibly suppose that eleven, which he is

---

47. 'I can't stand old Socrates, either, that chattering pauper, who has thought over everything else, but neglected to find out where he could get anything to eat.' (Eupolis fr. 352). 'Garrulousness' was one of the stock gibes of the comic poets against philosophers. Cp. *Phaedo* 70 c: 'No one—not even a comic poet—could accuse me of irrelevant chattering if he were listening now.'

merely thinking about, is twelve, which again he is merely thinking about?' Come now, you answer.

THEAET. Well, my answer will be that someone who is seeing or touching them could suppose that eleven are twelve, but not with those that he has in his thought: he would never judge this in that way about them.

SOC. Well, now, take the case where a man is considering five and seven within himself—I don't mean seven men and five men, or anything of that sort, but five and seven themselves; the records, as we allege, in that waxen block, things amongst which it is not possible that there should be false judgement. Suppose he is talking to himself about them, and asking himself how many they are. Do you think that in such a case it has ever happened that one man thought they were eleven and said so, while another thought and said that they were twelve? Or do all men say and all men think that they are twelve? *196*

THEAET. Oh, good Heavens, no; lots of people would make them eleven. And with larger numbers they go wrong still more often— for I suppose what you say is intended to apply to all numbers. *b*

SOC. Quite right. And I want you to consider whether what happens here is not just this, that a man thinks that twelve itself, the one on the waxen block, is eleven.

THEAET. It certainly looks as if he does.

SOC. Then haven't we come back to the things we were saying at the outset? You see, anyone to whom this happens is thinking that one thing he knows is another thing he knows. And this we said was impossible; in fact, it was just this consideration which led us to exclude the possibility of false judgement, because, if admitted, it would mean that the same man must, at one and the same time, both know and not know the same objects. *c*

THEAET. That's perfectly true.

SOC. Then we shall have to say that false judgement is something other than a misapplication of thought to perception; because if this were so, we could never be in error so long as we remained within our thoughts themselves. But as the matter now stands, either there is no such thing as false judgement; or a man may not know what he knows. Which do you choose?

THEAET. You are offering me an impossible choice, Socrates.

SOC. But I'm afraid the argument will not permit both. Still—we must stop at nothing; supposing now we were to set about being quite shameless? *d*

THEAET. How?

Soc. By consenting to say what knowing is like.

THEAET. And why should that be shameless?

Soc. You don't seem to realise that our whole discussion from the beginning has been an enquiry about knowledge, on the assumption that we do not yet know what it is.

THEAET. Oh, but I do.

Soc. Well, then, don't you think it is a shameless thing that we, who don't know what knowledge is, should pronounce on what *e* knowing is like? But as a matter of fact, Theaetetus, for some time past our whole method of discussion has been tainted. Time and again we have said 'we are acquainted with' and 'we are not acquainted with', 'we know' and 'we do not know', as if we could to some extent understand one another while we are still ignorant of what knowledge is. Or here's another example, if you like: at this very moment, we have again used the words 'to be ignorant of', and 'to understand', as if these were quite proper expressions for us when we are deprived of knowledge.

THEAET. But how are you going to carry on the discussion at all, Socrates, if you keep off these words?

197 Soc. Quite impossible, for a man like me; but if I were one of the experts in contradiction, I might be able to. If one of those gentlemen were present, he would have commanded us to refrain from them, and would keep coming down upon us heavily for the faults I'm referring to. But since we are no good anyway, why don't I make bold to tell you what knowing is like? It seems to me that this might be of some help.

THEAET. Then do be bold, please. And if you don't keep from using these words, we'll forgive you all right.

Soc. Well, then, have you heard what people are saying nowadays that knowing is?

THEAET. I dare say I have; but I don't remember it at the moment.

b Soc. Well, they say, of course, that it is 'the having of knowledge'.

THEAET. Oh, yes, that's true.

Soc. Let us make a slight change; let us say 'the possession of knowledge'.

THEAET. And how would you say that was different from the first way of putting it?

Soc. Perhaps it isn't at all; but I will tell you what I think the difference is, and then you must help me to examine it.

THEAET. All right—if I can.

Soc. Well, then, to 'possess' doesn't seem to me to be the same as to 'have'. For instance, suppose a man has bought a coat and it is at his disposal but he is not wearing it; we would not say that he 'has' it on, but we would say he 'possesses' it.[48]

THEAET. Yes, that would be correct.

Soc. Now look here: is it possible in this way to possess knowl-   c
edge and not 'have' it? Suppose a man were to hunt wild birds, pigeons or something, and make an aviary for them at his house and look after them there; then, in a sense, I suppose, we might say he 'has' them all the time, because of course he possesses them. Isn't that so?

THEAET. Yes.

Soc. But in another sense he 'has' none of them; it is only that he has acquired a certain power in respect of them, because he has got them under his control in an enclosure of his own. That is to say, he has the power to hunt for any one he likes at any time, and   d
take and 'have' it whenever he chooses, and let it go again; and this he can do as often as he likes.

THEAET. That is so.

Soc. Well a little while ago we were equipping souls with I don't know what sort of a waxen device. Now let us make in each soul a sort of aviary of all kinds of birds; some in flocks separate from the others, some in small groups, and others flying about singly here and there among all the rest.

THEAET. All right, let us suppose it made. What then?   e

Soc. Then we must say that when we are children this receptacle is empty; and by the birds we must understand pieces of knowl-edge. When anyone takes possession of a piece of knowledge and shuts it up in the pen, we should say that he has learned or has found out the thing of which this is the knowledge; and knowing, we should say, is this.

THEAET. That's given, then.

Soc. Now think: when he hunts again for any one of the pieces   198
of knowledge that he chooses, and takes it and 'has' it, then lets it go again, what words are appropriate here? The same as before, when he took possession of the knowledge, or different ones?— You will see my point more clearly in this way. There is an art you call arithmetic, isn't there?

THEAET. Yes.

---

48. The Greek verb for 'I have' can mean not only 'I possess', but also 'I have it on' (e.g. an article of clothing) or 'I have hold of it'.

Soc. Now I want you to think of this as a hunt for pieces of knowledge concerning everything odd and even.

THEAET. All right, I will.

b   Soc. It is by virtue of this art, I suppose, that a man both has under his control pieces of knowledge concerning numbers and also hands them over to others?

THEAET. Yes.

Soc. And we call it 'teaching' when a man hands them over to others, and 'learning' when he gets them handed over to him; and when he 'has' them through possessing them in this aviary of ours, we call that 'knowing'.

THEAET. Yes, certainly.

Soc. Now you must give your attention to what is coming next. It must surely be true that a man who has completely mastered arithmetic knows all numbers? Because there are pieces of knowledge covering all numbers in his soul.

THEAET. Of course.

c   Soc. And a man so trained may proceed to do some counting, either counting to himself the numbers themselves, or counting something else, one of the external things which have number?

THEAET. Yes, surely.

Soc. And counting we shall take to be simply a matter of considering how large a number actually is?

THEAET. Yes.

Soc. Then it looks as if this man were considering something which he knows as if he did not know it (for we have granted that he knows all numbers). I've no doubt you've had such puzzles put to you.

THEAET. I have, yes.

d   Soc. Then using our image of possessing and hunting for the pigeons, we shall say that there are two phases of hunting: one before you have possession, in order to get possession, and another when you already possess in order to catch and have in your hands what you previously acquired. And in this way even with things you learned and got the knowledge of long ago and have known ever since, it is possible to learn them—these same things—all over again. You can take up again and 'have' that knowledge of each of them which you acquired long ago but had not ready to hand in your thought, can't you?

THEAET. True.

e   Soc. Now this is what I meant by my question a moment ago. What terms ought we to use about them when we speak of what the arithmetician does when he proceeds to count, or the scholar when he proceeds to read something? Here, it seems, a man who knows something is setting out to learn again from himself things which he already knows.

THEAET. But that would be a very odd thing, Socrates.

Soc. But are we to say that it is things which he does not know that such a man is going to read and count—remembering that we *199* have granted him knowledge of all letters and all numbers?

THEAET. That wouldn't be reasonable, either.

Soc. Then would you like us to take this line? Suppose we say we do not mind at all about the names; let people drag around the terms 'knowing' and 'learning' to their heart's content. We have determined that to 'possess' knowledge is one thing and to 'have' it is another; accordingly we maintain that it is impossible for anyone not to possess that which he has possession of, and thus it never happens that he does not know something he knows. But he may yet make a false judgement about it. This is because it is possible for him to 'have', not the knowledge of this thing, but *b* another piece of knowledge instead. When he is hunting for one piece of knowledge, it may happen, as they fly about, that he makes a mistake and gets hold of one instead of another. It was this that happened when he thought eleven was twelve. He got hold of the knowledge of eleven that was in him, instead of the knowledge of twelve, as you might catch a ring-dove instead of a pigeon.

THEAET. Yes; that is reasonable, now.

Soc. But when he gets hold of the one he is trying to get hold of, then he is free from error; when he does that, he is judging what is. In this way, both true and false judgement exist; and the things that worried us before no longer stand in our way. I daresay you'll *c* agree with me? Or, if not, what line will you take?

THEAET. I agree.

Soc. Yes; we have now got rid of this 'not knowing what one knows'. For we now find that at no point does it happen that we do not possess what we possess, whether we are in error about anything or not. But it looks to me as if something else more alarming is by way of coming upon us.

THEAET. What's that?

Soc. I mean, what is involved if false judgement is going to become a matter of an interchange of pieces of knowledge.

THEAET. What do you mean?

Soc. To begin with, it follows that a man who has knowledge *d* of something is ignorant of this very thing not through want of knowledge but actually in virtue of his knowledge. Secondly, he judges that this is something else and that the other thing is it. Now surely this is utterly unreasonable; it means that the soul, when knowledge becomes present to it, knows nothing and is wholly ignorant. According to this argument, there is no reason why an accession of ignorance should not make one know something, or of blindness make one see something, if knowledge is ever going to make a man ignorant.

e   THEAET. Well, perhaps, Socrates, it wasn't a happy thought to make the birds only pieces of knowledge. Perhaps we ought to have supposed that there are pieces of ignorance also flying about in the soul along with them, and what happens is that the hunter sometimes catches a piece of knowledge and sometimes a piece of ignorance concerning the same thing; and the ignorance makes him judge falsely, while the knowledge makes him judge truly.

Soc. I can hardly refrain from expressing my admiration of you, Theaetetus; but do think again about that. Let us suppose it is as you say: then, you maintain, the man who catches a piece of igno-

200   rance will judge falsely. Is that it?

THEAET. Yes.

Soc. But presumably he will not think he is judging falsely?

THEAET. No, of course he won't.

Soc. He will think he is judging what is true; and his attitude towards the things about which he is in error will be as if he knew them.

THEAET. Of course.

Soc. He will think he has hunted down and 'has' a piece of knowledge and not a piece of ignorance.

THEAET. Yes, that's clear.

Soc. So, after going a long way round, we are back at our original difficulty. Our friend the expert in refutation will laugh. 'My very

b   good people,' he will say, 'do you mean that a man who knows both knowledge and ignorance is thinking that one of them which he knows is the other which he knows? Or is it that he knows neither, and judges the one he doesn't know to be the other which he doesn't know? Or is it that he knows one and not the other, and judges that the one he knows is the one he doesn't know? Or does he think that the one he doesn't know is the one he does? Or are you going to start all over again and tell me that there's another set of pieces of knowledge concerning pieces of knowledge and ignorance, which a man may possess shut up in some other ridicu-

c   lous aviaries or waxen devices, which he knows so long as he

possesses them though he may not have them ready to hand in his
soul—and in this way end up forced to come running round to the
same place over and over again and never get any further?' What
are we going to say to that, Theaetetus?

THEAET. Oh, dear me, Socrates, I don't know what one ought to
say.

Soc. Then don't you think, my boy, that the argument is perhaps
dealing out a little proper chastisement, and showing us that we
were wrong to leave the question about knowledge and proceed to
enquire into false judgement first? While as a matter of fact it's   *d*
impossible to know this until we have an adequate grasp of what
knowledge is.

THEAET. Well, at the moment, Socrates, I feel bound to believe
you.

Soc. Then, to go back to the beginning, what are we going to
say knowledge is?—We are not, I suppose, going to give up yet?

THEAET. Certainly not, unless you give up yourself.

Soc. Tell me, then, how could we define it with the least risk of
contradicting ourselves?

THEAET. In the way we were attempting before, Socrates; I can't   *e*
think of any other.

Soc. In what way do you mean?

THEAET. By saying that knowledge is true judgement. Judging
truly is at least something free of mistakes, I take it, and everything
that results from it is admirable and good.

Soc. Well, Theaetetus, as the man who was leading the way
across the river said, 'It will show you.'[49] If we go on and track this
down, perhaps we may stumble on what we are looking for; if we   *201*
stay where we are, nothing will come clear.

THEAET. You're right; let's go on and consider it.

Soc. Well, this won't take long to consider, anyway; there is a
whole art indicating to you that knowledge is not what you say.

THEAET. How's that? What art do you mean?

Soc. The art of the greatest representatives of wisdom— the men
called orators and lawyers. These men, I take it, use their art to
produce conviction not by teaching people, but by making them
judge whatever they themselves choose. Or do you think there are

49. According to the scholiast the story was: some travellers came to the bank of a
river, which they wished to cross at the ford; one of them asked the guide, 'Is the
water deep?' He said, 'It will show you', i.e. don't ask the guide, you must try it for
yourself.

b   any teachers so clever that within the short time allowed by the
clock they can teach adequately the truth of what happened to
people who have been robbed or assaulted, in a case where there
were no eye-witnesses?

THEAET. No, I don't think they possibly could; but they might
be able to *persuade* them.

Soc. And by 'persuading them', you mean 'causing them to
judge', don't you?

THEAET. Of course.

Soc. Then suppose a jury has been justly persuaded of some
matter which only an eye-witness could know, and which cannot
otherwise be known; suppose they come to their decision upon
c   hearsay, forming a true judgement: then they have decided the
case without knowledge, but, granted they did their job well, being
correctly persuaded?

THEAET. Yes, certainly.

Soc. But, my dear lad, they couldn't have done that if true judgement is the same thing as knowledge; in that case the best juryman
in the world couldn't form a correct judgement without knowledge.
So it seems they must be different things.

THEAET. Oh, yes, Socrates, that's just what I once heard a man
say; I had forgotten, but now it's coming back to me. He said
d   that it is true judgement with an account[50] that is knowledge; true
judgement without an account falls outside of knowledge. And he
said that the things of which there is no account are not knowable
(yes, he actually called them that),[51] while those which have an
account are knowable.

Soc. Very good indeed. Now tell me, how did he distinguish
these knowables and unknowables? I want to see if you and I have
heard the same version.

THEAET. I don't know if I can find that out; but I think I could
follow if someone explained it.

Soc. Listen then to a dream in return for a dream. In my dream,
e   too, I thought I was listening to people saying that the primary
elements, as it were, of which we and everything else are composed, have no account. Each of them, in itself, can only be named;

50. 'Account' translates *logos*, on which see Introduction, p. 134.

51. The parenthesis may alternatively be translated: '(that was the word he used)'.
The translation in the text expresses surprise about the claim that some things are
not knowable at all. The alternative translation calls attention to the particular Greek
word used for 'knowable'.

it is not possible to say anything else of it, either that it is[52] or that
it is not. That would mean that we were adding being or not-being   202
to it; whereas we must not attach anything, if we are to speak of
that thing itself alone. Indeed we ought not to apply to it even such
words as 'itself' or 'that', 'each', 'alone', or 'this', or any other of
the many words of this kind; for these go the round and are applied
to all things alike, being other than the things to which they are
added, whereas if it were possible to express the element itself and
it had its own proprietary account, it would have to be expressed
without any other thing. As it is, however, it is impossible that any
of the primaries should be expressed in an account; it can only be   b
named, for a name is all that it has. But with the things composed
of these, it is another matter. Here, just in the same way as the
elements themselves are woven together, so their names may be
woven together and become an account of something—an account
being essentially a complex[53] of names. Thus the elements are unaccountable and unknowable, but they are perceivable, whereas the
complexes are both knowable and expressible and can be the objects
of true judgement.

Now when a man gets a true judgement about something without
an account, his soul is in a state of truth as regards that thing, but   c
he does not know it; for someone who cannot give and take an
account of a thing is ignorant about it. But when he has also got an
account of it, he is capable of all this and is made perfect in knowledge. Was the dream you heard the same as this or a different one?

THEAET. No, it was the same in every respect.

Soc. Do you like this then, and do you suggest that knowledge
is true judgement with an account?

THEAET. Yes, certainly.

Soc. Theaetetus, can it be that all in a moment, you and I have   d
today laid hands upon something which many a wise man has
searched for in the past—and gone grey before he found it?

---

52. The translation is intended to leave it unclear, as the original is unclear, whether
'anything else' refers here to the statement that it is, or to anything it might be said
to be. The two construals come to much the same if the first is understood, as it
probably ought to be, not as the statement that it exists, but as the incomplete initial
portion of a statement saying that it is something or other. The whole sentence could
then be printed thus: 'it is not possible to say anything else of it, either that it is . . .
or that it is not . . .'.

53. Literally, 'a weaving together'—the Greek noun *sumplokē*, like the English word
'complex' itself, is related to the verb translated 'woven together' in the previous
two lines.

THEAET. Well, it does seem to me anyway, Socrates, that what has just been said puts the matter very well.

Soc. And it seems likely enough that the matter is really so; for what knowledge could there be apart from an account and correct judgement? But there is one of the things said which I don't like.

THEAET. And what's that?

Soc. What looks like the subtlest point of all—that the elements *e* are unknowable and the complexes knowable.

THEAET. And won't that do?

Soc. We must make sure; because, you see, we do have as hostages for this theory the original models that were used when all these statements were made.

THEAET. What models?

Soc. Letters—the elements of language—and syllables.[54] It must have been these, mustn't it, that the author of our theory had in view—it couldn't have been anything else?

THEAET. No, he must have been thinking of letters and syllables.

203   Soc. Let's take and examine them then. Or rather let us examine ourselves, and ask ourselves whether we really learned our letters in this way or not. Now, to begin with, one can give an account of the syllables but not of the letters—is that it?

THEAET. Well, perhaps.

Soc. It most certainly looks like that to me. At any rate, supposing you were asked about the first syllable of 'Socrates': 'Tell me, Theaetetus, what is SO?' What would you answer to that?

THEAET. That it's S and O.[55]

Soc. And there you have an account of the syllable?

THEAET. Yes.

b   Soc. Come along then, and let us have the account of S in the same way.

THEAET. How *can* anyone give the letters of a letter? S is just one

---

54. The Greek words used in a general sense for 'elements' and 'complexes' are also regularly used for 'letters' and 'syllables'. Thus one word, *stoicheion*, is translated 'element' when the context is general (as above, 201e) and 'letter' when the reference is to linguistic elements; and one word, *sullabē*, is translated 'complex' when the context is general (as above, 202b) and 'syllable' when the reference is to complexes of letters. A third word, *grammata*, meaning 'letters' or language in general, is used here and at 203a, 204a, 206a, 207de, to specify when 'element' and 'complex' are to be taken linguistically and when generally.

'Letter' must be understood throughout the discussion as covering both written letters and the sounds (phonemes) which written letters represent.

55. Theaetetus actually says, 'That it's sigma and omega', using the names of the *Greek* letters in Socrates' name.

of the voiceless letters, Socrates, a mere sound like a hissing of the tongue. B again has neither voice nor sound, and that's true of most letters. So the statement that they themselves are unaccountable holds perfectly good. Even the seven clearest have only voice; no sort of account whatever can be given of them.[56]

Soc. So here, my friend, we have established a point about knowledge.

Theaet. We do appear to have done so.

Soc. Well then: we have shown that the syllable is knowable but not the letter—is that all right?

Theaet. It seems the natural conclusion, anyway.

Soc. Look here, what do we mean by 'the syllable'? The two letters (or if there are more, all the letters)? Or do we mean some single form produced by their combination?

Theaet. I think we mean all the letters.

Soc. Then take the case of the two letters, S and O; these two are the first syllable of my name. If a man knows the syllable, he must know both the letters?

Theaet. Of course.

Soc. So he knows S and O.

Theaet. Yes.

Soc. But can it be that he is ignorant of each one, and knows the two of them without knowing either?

Theaet. That would be a strange and unaccountable thing, Socrates.

Soc. And yet, supposing it is necessary to know each in order to know both, then it is absolutely necessary that anyone who is ever to know a syllable must first get to know the letters. And in admitting this, we shall find that our beautiful theory has taken to its heels and got clean away from us.

Theaet. And very suddenly too.

Soc. Yes; we are not keeping a proper watch on it. Perhaps we ought not to have supposed the syllable to be the letters; perhaps we ought to have made it some single form produced out of them, having its own single nature—something different from the letters.

Theaet. Yes, certainly; that might be more like it.

Soc. We must look into the matter; we have no right to betray a great and imposing theory in this faint-hearted manner.

---

56. The 'seven' are the seven vowels of ancient Greek, as contrasted with two classes of consonant: mutes like B, which cannot be pronounced without a vowel, and semivowels like S, which can.

THEAET. Certainly not.

204

Soc. Then let it be as we are now suggesting. Let the complex be a single form resulting from the combination of the several elements when they fit together; and let this hold both of language and of things in general.

THEAET. Yes, certainly.

Soc. Then it must have no parts.

THEAET. Why is that, now?

Soc. Because when a thing has parts, the whole is necessarily all the parts. Or do you mean by 'the whole' also a single form arising out of the parts, yet different from all the parts?

THEAET. I do.

Soc. Now do you call 'sum'[57] and 'whole' the same thing or

b different things?

THEAET. I don't feel at all certain; but as you keep telling me to answer up with a good will, I will take a risk and say they are different.

Soc. Your good will, Theaetetus, is all that it should be. Now we must see if your answer is too.

THEAET. We must, of course.

Soc. As the argument stands at present, the whole will be different from the sum?

THEAET. Yes.

Soc. Well now, is there any difference between all the things and the sum? For instance, when we say 'one, two, three, four,

c five, six'; or, 'twice three', or 'three times two', 'four and two', 'three and two and one'; are we speaking of the same thing in all these cases or different things?

THEAET. The same thing.

Soc. That is, six?

THEAET. Precisely.

Soc. Then with each expression have we not spoken of all the six?

THEAET. Yes.

Soc. And when we speak of them all, aren't we speaking of a sum?

THEAET. We must be.

Soc. That is, six?

THEAET. Precisely.

---

57. The word translated 'sum' (*pan*) and the word translated 'all' (*panta*) in the phrase 'all the parts' are singular and plural forms of the same Greek word.

Soc. Then in all things made up of number, at any rate, by 'the   *d*
sum' and 'all of them' we mean the same thing?

Theaet. So it seems.

Soc. Now let us talk about them in this way. The number of an
acre is the same thing as an acre, isn't it?

Theaet. Yes.

Soc. Similarly with a mile.

Theaet. Yes.

Soc. And the number of an army is the same as the army? And
so always with things of this sort; their total number is the sum that
each of them is.

Theaet. Yes.

Soc. But is the number of each anything other than its parts?   *e*

Theaet. No.

Soc. Now things which have parts consist of parts?

Theaet. That seems true.

Soc. And it is agreed that all the parts are the sum, seeing that
the total number is to be the sum.

Theaet. That is so.

Soc. Then the whole does not consist of parts. For if it did, it
would be all the parts and so would be a sum.

Theaet. It looks as if it doesn't.

Soc. But can a part, as such, be a part of anything but the whole?

Theaet. Yes; of the sum.

Soc. You are putting up a good fight anyway, Theaetetus. But   *205*
this sum now—isn't it just when there is nothing lacking that it is
a sum?

Theaet. Yes, necessarily.

Soc. And won't this very same thing—that from which nothing
anywhere is lacking—be a whole? While a thing from which something is absent is neither a whole nor a sum—the same consequence
having followed from the same condition in both cases at once?

Theaet. Well, it doesn't seem to me now that there can be any
difference between whole and sum.

Soc. Very well. Now were we not saying[58] that in the case of a
thing that has parts, both the whole and the sum will be all the
parts?

Theaet. Yes, certainly.

Soc. Now come back to the thing I was trying to get at just now.
Supposing the syllable is not just its letters, doesn't it follow that it   *b*

58. At 204a.

cannot contain the letters as parts of itself? Alternatively, if it is the same as the letters, it must be equally knowable with them?

Theaet. That is so.

Soc. Well, wasn't it just in order to avoid this result that we supposed it different from the letters?

Theaet. Yes.

Soc. Well then, if the letters are not parts of the syllable, can you tell me of any other things, not its letters, which are?

Theaet. No, indeed. If I were to admit that it had component parts, Socrates, it would be ridiculous, of course, to set aside the letters and look for other components.

c   Soc. Then, Theaetetus, according to our present argument, a syllable is an absolutely single form, indivisible into parts.

Theaet. It looks like it.

Soc. Now, my friend, a little while ago, if you remember, we were inclined to accept a certain proposition which we thought put the matter very well—I mean the statement that no account can be given of the primaries of which other things are constituted, because each of them is in itself incomposite; and that it would be incorrect to apply even the term 'being' to it when we spoke of it or the term 'this', because these terms signify different and alien things; and that is the reason why a primary is an unaccountable and unknowable thing. Do you remember?

Theaet. I remember.

d   Soc. And is that the reason also why it is single in form and indivisible into parts or is there some other reason for that? I can see no other myself.

Theaet. No, there really doesn't seem to be any other.

Soc. And hasn't the complex now fallen into the same class as the primary, seeing it has no parts and is a single form?

Theaet. Yes, it certainly has.

Soc. Well now, if the complex is both many elements and a whole, with them as its parts, then both complexes and elements are equally capable of being known and expressed, since all the parts turned out to be the same thing as the whole.

e   Theaet. Yes, surely.

Soc. But if, on the other hand, the complex is single and without parts, then complexes and elements are equally unaccountable and unknowable—both of them for the same reason.

Theaet. I can't dispute that.

Soc. Then if anyone tries to tell us that the complex can be known and expressed, while the contrary is true of the element, we had better not listen to him.

THEAET. No, we'd better not, if we go along with the argument.

Soc. And, more than this, wouldn't you more easily believe   206
somebody who made the contrary statement, because of what you
know of your own experience in learning to read and write?

THEAET. What kind of thing do you mean?

Soc. I mean that when you were learning you spent your time
just precisely in trying to distinguish, by both eye and ear, each
individual letter in itself so that you might not be bewildered by
their different positions in written and spoken words.

THEAET. That's perfectly true.

Soc. And at the music-teacher's, wasn't the finished pupil the one
who could follow each note and tell to which string it belonged—the   b
notes being generally admitted to be the elements in music?

THEAET. Yes, that's just what it amounted to.

Soc. Then if the proper procedure is to take such elements and
complexes as we ourselves have experience of, and make an infer-
ence from them to the rest, we shall say that the elements are much
more clearly known, and the knowledge of them is more decisive
for the mastery of any branch of study than knowledge of the
complex. And if anyone maintains that the complex is by nature
knowable, and the element unknowable, we shall regard this as
tomfoolery, whether it is intended to be or not.

THEAET. Oh, quite.

Soc. I think that might be proved in other ways too. But we   c
mustn't let them distract us from the problem before us. We wanted
to see what can be meant by the proposition that it is in the addition
of an account to a true judgement that knowledge is perfected.

THEAET. Well yes, we must try to see that.

Soc. Come then, what are we intended to understand by an
'account'? I think it must be one of three meanings.

THEAET. What are they?

Soc. The first would be, making one's thought apparent vocally   d
by means of words and verbal expressions—when a man impresses
an image of his judgement upon the stream of speech, like reflec-
tions upon water or in a mirror. Don't you think this kind of thing
is an account?

THEAET. Yes, I do. At least, a man who does this is said to be
giving an account.[59]

Soc. But isn't that a thing that everyone is able to do more or

---

59. 'Giving an account' here translates *legein*, the ordinary Greek word for 'say,
speak, speak of', which corresponds to *logos* in its wider meanings 'speech, dis-
course, statement'.

less readily—I mean, indicate what he thinks about a thing, if he is not deaf or dumb to begin with? And that being so, anyone at all who makes a correct judgement will turn out to have it 'together with an account'; correct judgement without knowledge will no longer be found anywhere.

THEAET. True.

Soc. Well then, we mustn't be too ready to condemn the author of the definition of knowledge now before us for talking nonsense. Perhaps he didn't mean this; perhaps he meant being able, when questioned about what a thing is, to give an answer by reference to its elements.

THEAET. As for example, Socrates?

Soc. As for example, what Hesiod is doing when he says 'One hundred are the timbers of a wagon.'[60] Now I couldn't say what they are; and I don't suppose you could either. If you and I were asked what a wagon is, we should be satisfied if we could answer, 'Wheels, axle, body, rails, yoke.'

THEAET. Yes, surely.

Soc. But he might think us ridiculous, just as he would if we were asked what your name is, and replied by giving the syllables. In that case, he would think us ridiculous because although we might be correct in our judgement and our expression of it, we should be fancying ourselves as scholars, thinking we knew and were expressing a scholar's account of Theaetetus' name. Whereas in fact no one gives an account of a thing with knowledge till, in addition to his true judgement, he goes right through the thing element by element—as I think we said before.

THEAET. We did, yes.

Soc. In the same way, in the example of the wagon, he would say that we have indeed correct judgement; but it is the man who can explore its being by going through those hundred items who has made the addition which adds an account to his true judgement. It is this man who has passed from mere judgement to expert knowledge of the being of a wagon; and he has done so in virtue of having gone over the whole by means of the elements.

THEAET. And doesn't that seem sound to you, Socrates?

Soc. Well, tell me if it seems sound to you, my friend. Tell me if you are prepared to accept the view that an account is a matter of going through a thing element by element, while going through it by 'syllables' or larger divisions falls short of being an account. Then we shall be able to discuss it.

60. Hesiod, *Works and Days* 456.

THEAET. I'm certainly prepared to accept that.

Soc. And do you at the same time think that a man has knowledge of anything when he believes the same thing now to be part of one thing and now part of something else? Or when he judges that now one thing and now something different belongs to one and the same object?

THEAET. No, indeed I don't.

Soc. Then have you forgotten that at first when you were learning to read and write that is just what you and the other boys used to do?

THEAET. You mean we used to think that sometimes one letter and sometimes another belonged to the same syllable, and used to put the same letter sometimes into its proper syllable and sometimes into another?

e

Soc. Yes, that is what I mean.

THEAET. Well, I certainly haven't forgotten; and I don't think people at that stage can be said to have knowledge yet.

Soc. Well, suppose now that someone who is at this sort of stage is writing the name 'Theaetetus'; he thinks he ought to write THE and does so.[61] Then suppose another time he is trying to write 'Theodorus', and this time he thinks he should write TE and proceeds to do so. Are we going to say that he knows the first syllable of your names?

208

THEAET. No. We've admitted that anyone who is at that stage has not yet knowledge.

Soc. And is there anything to prevent the same person being in that situation as regards the second and third and fourth syllables?

THEAET. No, nothing.

Soc. Now at the time when he does this, he will be writing 'Theaetetus' not only with correct judgement, but with command of the way through its letters; that must be so whenever he writes them out one after another in their order.

THEAET. Yes, clearly.

Soc. And still without knowledge though with correct judgement—isn't that our view?

b

THEAET. Yes.

Soc. Yet possessing an account of it along with his correct judgement. He was writing it, you see, with command of the way through its letters; and we agreed that that is an account.

---

61. Socrates actually says, 'he thinks he ought to write theta and epsilon', using the names of the *Greek* letters in the first syllable of Theaetetus' name. There are only two such letters because Greek represents the sound of TH by the single letter theta.

THEAET. True.

Soc. So here, my friend, we have correct judgement together with an account, which we are not yet entitled to call knowledge.

THEAET. Yes, I'm afraid that's so.

Soc. So it was only the poor man's dream of gold that we had when we thought we had got the truest account of knowledge. Or is it early days to be harsh? Perhaps this is not the way in which one is to define 'account'. We said that the man who defines knowledge as correct judgement together with an account would choose one of three meanings for 'account'. Perhaps the last is the one to define it by.

THEAET. Yes, you're right to remind me; there is one possibility still left. The first was, a kind of vocal image of thought; the one we have just discussed was the way to the whole through the elements. Now what's your third suggestion?

Soc. What the majority of people would say—namely, being able to tell some mark by which the object you are asked about differs from all other things.

THEAET. Can you give me an example of such an 'account' of something?

Soc. Well, take the sun, if you like. You would be satisfied, I imagine, with the answer that it is the brightest of the bodies that move round the earth in the heavens.

THEAET. Oh yes, quite.

Soc. Now I want you to get hold of the principle that this illustrates. It is what we were just saying—that if you get hold of the difference that distinguishes a thing from everything else, then, so some people say, you will have got an account of it. On the other hand, so long as it is some common feature that you grasp, your account will be about all those things which have this in common.

THEAET. I see; I think it's very good to call this kind of thing an account.

Soc. Then if a man with correct judgement about any one of the things that are grasps in addition its difference from the rest, he has become a knower of the thing he was a judger of before.

THEAET. That's our present position, anyway.

Soc. Well, at this point, Theaetetus, as regards what we are saying, I'm for all the world like a man looking at a shadow-painting;[62]

Moreover, this sound was a plosive (as in English *fathead*), rather than a fricative (as in English *thin*), and so easy enough to confuse with TE.

62. The pictorial technique referred to (*skiagraphia*) seems to have been one which depended on contrasts between light and shade to create the appearance of form

when I'm close up to it I can't take it in in the least, though when I
stood well back from it, it appeared to me to have some meaning.

THEAET. How's that?

Soc. I'll see if I can explain. Suppose I have formed a correct   *209*
judgement about you; if I can grasp your account in addition, I
know you, but if not, I am merely judging.

THEAET. Yes.

Soc. And an account was to be a matter of expounding your
differentness?

THEAET. That is so.

Soc. Then when I was merely judging, my thought failed to
grasp any point of difference between you and the rest of mankind?

THEAET. Apparently.

Soc. What I had in mind, it seems, was some common characteristic—something that belongs no more to you than to anybody else.

THEAET. Yes, that must be so.   *b*

Soc. Then tell me, in Heaven's name how, if that was so, did it
come about that you were the object of my judgement and nobody
else? Suppose my thought is that 'This is Theaetetus—one who is
a human being, and has a nose and eyes and mouth', and so on
through the whole list of limbs. Will this thought cause me to be
thinking of Theaetetus rather than of Theodorus, or of the proverbial 'remotest Mysian'?

THEAET. No, how could it?

Soc. But suppose I think not merely of 'the one with nose and
eyes', but of 'the one with a snub nose and prominent eyes'. Shall   *c*
I even then be judging about you any more than about myself or
anyone who is like that?

THEAET. Not at all.

Soc. It will not, I take it, be Theaetetus who is judged in my
mind until this snub-nosedness of yours has left imprinted and
established in me a record that is different in some way from the
other snub-nosednesses I have seen; and so with the other details
of your make-up. And this will remind me, if I meet you to-morrow,
and make me judge correctly about you.

THEAET. That's perfectly true.

Soc. Then correct judgement also must be concerned with the   *d*
differentness of what it is about?

THEAET. So it seems, anyway.

Soc. Then what more might this 'adding an account to correct

---

and volume. A more familiar comparison for modern readers would be a pointilliste
painting by Seurat.

judgement' be? If, on the one hand, it means that we must make another judgement about the way in which a thing differs from the rest of things, we are being required to do something very absurd.

THEAET. How's that?

Soc. Because we already have a correct judgement about the way a thing differs from other things; and we are then directed to add a correct judgement about the way it differs from other things. At that rate, the way a roller goes round or a pestle or anything else *e* proverbial would be nothing compared with such directions; they might be more justly called a matter of 'the blind leading the blind'. To tell us to add what we already have, in order to come to know what we are judging about, bears a generous resemblance to the behaviour of a man benighted.

THEAET. Whereas if, on the other hand, . . . ? What else were you going to suggest when you started this enquiry just now?

Soc. Well, if 'adding an account' means that we are required to get to *know* the differentness, not merely judge it, this most splendid of our accounts of knowledge turns out to be a very amusing affair. *210* For getting to know of course is acquiring knowledge, isn't it?

THEAET. Yes.

Soc. So, it seems, the answer to the question 'What is knowledge?' will be 'Correct judgement accompanied by *knowledge* of the differentness'—for this is what we are asked to understand by the 'addition of an account'.

THEAET. Apparently so.

Soc. And it is surely just silly to tell us, when we are trying to discover what knowledge is, that it is correct judgement accompanied by *knowledge*, whether of differentness or of anything else? And so, Theaetetus, knowledge is neither perception nor true *b* judgement, nor an account added to true judgement.

THEAET. It seems not.

Soc. Well now, dear lad, are we still pregnant, still in labour with any thoughts about knowledge? Or have we been delivered of them all?

THEAET. As far as I'm concerned, Socrates, you've made me say far more than ever was in me, Heaven knows.

Soc. Well then, our art of midwifery tells us that all of these offspring are wind-eggs and not worth bringing up?

THEAET. Undoubtedly.

Soc. And so, Theaetetus, if ever in the future you should attempt *c* to conceive or should succeed in conceiving other theories, they will be better ones as the result of this enquiry. And if you remain

barren, your companions will find you gentler and less tiresome;
you will be modest and not think you know what you don't know.
This is all my art can achieve—nothing more. I do not know any of
the things that other men know—the great and inspired men of today and yesterday. But this art of midwifery my mother and I had
allotted to us by God; she to deliver women, I to deliver men that
are young and generous of spirit, all that have any beauty. And   *d*
now I must go to the King's Porch to meet the indictment that
Meletus has brought against me; but let us meet here again in the
morning, Theodorus.